TABLE OF CONTENTS

3

(From recent ALL INDIA, DNB, AIIMS, PGI, and JIPMER EXAMS)

Physiology

1) Normal dead space to tidal volume ratio
    a. 0.15
    b. 0.28
    c. 0.58
    d. 1.2

   Ans: (b)

Dead space (Vd) = 150 mL
Tidal volume (Vt) = 500mL.
Normal Vd/Vt ranges from approximately 0.28 to 0.33.

2) Respiratory parameter that does not change during pregnancy:
    a. Respiratory rate
    b. Tidal volume
    c. Expiratory reserve volume
    d. Residual volume

   Ans: (a)

Pregnant women experience nasal stuffiness due to estrogen-induced hypersecretion of mucus. Epistaxis is also common as a result of increased blood flow to the nasopharynx. The safest treatment of these symptoms is a saline nasal spray.

Pregnancy is a state of relative hyperventilation. An increased tidal volume with an unchanged respiratory rate leads to an increase in minute alveolar ventilation. This leads to respiratory alkalosis. The renal system compensates by increasing excretion of bicarbonate.

1. Respiratory rate does not change.
2. Tidal volume increases 0.1-0.2 L, about 40%.
3. Expiratory reserve volume decreases 15%.
4. Residual volume decreases.
5. Vital capacity does not change.
6. Inspiratory capacity increases 5%.
7. Functional reserve capacity decreases 18%.
8. Minute volume increases 40%.
9. Forced expiratory volume (FEV1) does not change.
10. PaO2 levels increase, from 100 to 110 mmHg.
11. PaCO2 levels decrease, from 40 to 27-32 mmHg.

3) True regarding hypoxemia- Multiple correct answers
    a. Decrease in ventilation
    b. Decrease in delivery of oxygen to tissues
    c. Inadequate utilization of oxygen by tissues despite normal delivery of oxygen
    d. Decreased oxygen pressure in blood
    e. All the above

Ans: (a & d)

Hypoxia is O2 deficiency at the tissue level. There are four categories:
1. Hypoxemia (hypoxic hypoxia) - low arterial oxygen tension (PaO2 <60 mm Hg)
2. Anemic hypoxia - arterial Po2 is normal but the amount of hemoglobin available to carry O2 is reduced
3. Ischemic or stagnant hypoxia - blood flow to a tissue is so low that adequate O2 is not delivered to it despite a normal Po2 and hemoglobin concentration
4. Histotoxic hypoxia - the amount of O2 delivered to a tissue is adequate but, because of the action of a toxic agent, the tissue cells cannot make use of the O2 supplied to them.

Hypoxemia is the most common form of hypoxia seen clinically. A PaO_2 of 60 mm Hg approximately corresponds SaO_2 of 90%. Further decreases in oxygen tension causes dramatic falls in hemoglobin saturation and resultant inadequate oxygen delivery to tissues.

Five causes of hypoxia

---

1. Hypoventilation
2. Ventilation/perfusion (V/Q) mismatch
3. Right to left shunt
4. Diffusion abnormalities
5. Reduced inspired oxygen tension.

Ventilation–perfusion imbalance is by far the most common cause of hypoxemia.

Hypoxemia from hypoventilation alone has an increased $PaCO_2$ and a normal A-a O_2 gradient.

4) Which ion stimulates peripheral chemoreceptors in hypoxia?
   a. Na^+
   b. K^+
   c. Cl^-
   d. Ca^{2+}

Ans: (b)

Peripheral chemoreceptor reflex

Peripheral arterial chemoreceptors in the carotid and aortic bodies are primarily activated by a reduction in arterial partial pressure of oxygen (PaO_2); they also respond to an increase in the arterial partial pressure of carbon dioxide ($PaCO_2$) and pH. A reduction in arterial PO_2 stimulates the carotid bodies. This stimulus causes an increase in ventilation. The increase in ventilation produces a fall in arterial PCO_2. The resultant hypocapnia will decrease the sensory output from carotid chemoreceptors.

9

Normally, even small reductions in arterial PO2 increases carotid chemoreceptor discharge, but only slightly. Significant increases in chemoreceptive activity do not occur until the arterial PO2 has fallen below 75 mm Hg. Ventilation increases markedly as PO2 falls below 60 mm Hg.

Each carotid and aortic body contains two types of cells, type 1 and type 2 cells. Type 1 cells are called glomus cells. They contain catecholamine. The catecholamine is released when there is hypoxia. It stimulates carotid sinus nerve fibers, which go through glossopharyngeal nerve. The type 2 cell surrounds four to six type 1 cells. Their function is probably supportive.

Type 1 glomus cells have oxygen sensitive K+ channels. *Oxygen interacts directly with cell membrane-bound potassium channels.* A decrease in PO2 closes potassium channels leading to depolarization of the type 1 cells and the generation of action potentials. The action potentials open voltage-gated calcium channels. Calcium ions enter the cell causing a rise in intracellular calcium ions. Elevation of intracellular calcium ions lead to neurotransmitter (catecholamine) exocytosis. This depolarizes the surrounding carotid sensory nerve terminal.

5) Hyperventilation is produced when PaCO2 is:
    a. < 35mmHg
    b. < 45mmHg
    c. > 40mmHg
    d. > 30mmHg

Ans: (c)

The arterial Pco2 is normally maintained at 40 mm Hg. When arterial Pco2 rises, ventilation is stimulated and the rate of pulmonary excretion of CO_2 increases until the arterial Pco2 falls to normal, shutting off the stimulus.

The chemoreceptors that mediate the hyperventilation produced by increases in arterial Pco2 are located in the medulla oblongata. The CO2 that enters the brain and CSF is promptly hydrated to H_2CO_3. The H_2CO_3 dissociates to H+ and HOC_3, so that the local H+ concentration rises. The H+ concentration in brain interstitial fluid parallels the arterial Pco2. Any increase in spinal fluid H+ concentration stimulates respiration. The magnitude of the stimulation is proportional to the rise in H+ concentration. Thus, the effects of CO_2 on respiration are mainly due to its movement into the CSF and brain interstitial fluid, where it increases the H+ concentration and stimulates receptors sensitive to H+.

6) True about infinite ventilation perfusion ratio -
   a. Partial pressure of oxygen in alveoli is same as in blood
   b. Partial pressure of oxygen in alveoli is same as in atmosphere
   c. There is absolute shunt
   d. There is relative dead space

Ans: (b)

The ventilation-perfusion ratio is the ratio between the amount of air getting to the alveoli (the alveolar ventilation, V, in ml/min) and the amount of blood being sent to the lungs (the cardiac output or Q - also in ml/min). Normal ventilation/perfusion ratio for the whole lung is 0.8 (4.2 L/min ventilation is divided by 5.5 L/ min of blood flow.) If perfusion is reduced relative to ventilation, alveolar PO2 rises because less oxygen diffuses from alveoli into blood and alveolar PCO2 falls because less CO2 diffuses from the blood into the alveoli. Alveoli with no ventilation (ratio of 0) have Po2 and Pco2 values that are the same as those of mixed venous blood because the trapped air in the unventilated alveoli equilibrates with mixed venous blood. Alveoli with no perfusion (ratio of Infinity) have Po2 and Pco2 values that are the same as inspired gas (ie, atmospheric air) because there is no gas exchange to alter the composition of the alveolar gas.

7) All shift oxygen dissociation curve to right except-
   a. Acidosis
   b. Hypocapnia
   c. Increased temperature
   d. Increased 2,3 DPG

Ans: (b)

A rightward shift indicates that the affinity of oxygen for hemoglobin is reduced. See figure below.

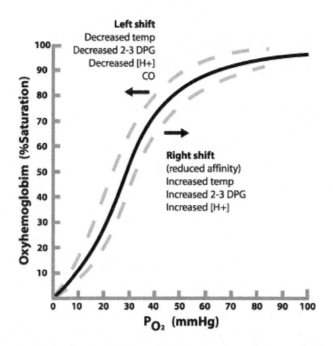

The upper portion is almost flat. This means that a fall of 20 to 30 mm Hg in arterial PO2 in a healthy subject with an initially normal value (about 100 mm Hg) causes only a minor reduction in arterial oxygen concentration. The steep lower part of the oxygen dissociation curve means that considerable amounts of oxygen can be unloaded to the peripheral tissues with only a relatively small drop in PO2.

When the curve is shifted to the right, a higher PO2 is needed for Hb to bind a given amount of oxygen. The oxygen dissociation curve is shifted to the right by an increase of temperature, hydrogen ion

12

concentration (fall in pH), PCO2, and concentration of 2, 3-diphosphoglycerate in the red cell.

8) What will be the PaO_2 after giving FiO_2 at 0.5 in a normal person?
   a. > 50 mmHg
   b. > 100 mmHg
   c. > 150 mmHg
   d. > 200 mmHg

Ans: (d)

Oxygen is carried in the blood in two forms. Arterial blood contains 20 mL of oxygen per dL – 19.7 mL bound to Hb and 0. 3 mL in dissolved form. The partial pressure of oxygen in blood is due to oxygen molecules dissolved in plasma (i.e., not bound to hemoglobin). *PaO2 reflects only free oxygen molecules dissolved in plasma and not those bound to hemoglobin.* Dissolved oxygen becomes important when a patient is given 100% oxygen to breathe. This raises the alveolar PO2 to over 600 mm Hg. If the lungs are normal, the dissolved oxygen may increase from 0.3 to 2 mL/100 mL blood.

FiO2 is the fraction of inspired oxygen (0.21 at room air). The atmospheric air that we inhale on a day to day basis is made up of 21% oxygen, 78% nitrogen and 1% trace elements such as argon, carbon dioxide, neon, helium, and methane. Thus, a patient on room air is breathing 21% oxygen and the PaO2 would be 100 mmHg. A patient on 100% oxygen should have a PaO2 of 500 mmHg. FiO2 of 0.5 means the person is inhaling 50 percent O2. A patient on 50% FIO2 should have a PaO2 of 250 mmHg. FiO2 is typically maintained below 0.5 even with mechanical ventilation, to avoid oxygen toxicity.

The expected Pao2 for a patient being given supplemental oxygen can be roughly estimated by multiplying the actual delivered percentage of O2 by 5, the "Five Times Rule." Thus, a patient getting 60% O2 would be expected to have a Pao2 of about 60 × 5, or 300 mm Hg.

13

9) Maximum forced expiration is primarily controlled by:
   a. Chest wall elasticity
   b. Diaphragm muscles
   c. Abdominal muscles
   d. Internal intercostal muscles

Ans: (c)

The volume expelled by an active expiratory effort after passive expiration is the expiratory reserve volume (1 L); the air left in the lungs after a maximal expiratory effort is the residual volume (1.3 L).

The vital capacity (3.5 L) is the largest amount of air that can be expired after a maximal inspiratory effort (this represents TV + IRV + ERV). It gives useful information about the strength of the respiratory muscles.

Lab tests

10) Functional residual capacity is the volume of air in the lung at the end of -----------
   a. Forced inspiration
   b. Normal inspiration
   c. Forced expiration
   d. Normal expiration

Ans: (d)

Functional residual capacity is the amount of air remaining in the lungs after a normal passive expiration. Functional residual capacity includes ERV+RV. FRC can be markedly affected by changes in posture. In the supine posture, the weight of the abdomen on the diaphragm has an expiratory effect. Therefore, end-expiratory lung volume falls. FRC is greatest when one is in the hands-and-knees position because the action of gravity is inspiratory on both rib cage and abdomen. Application of external forces, such as immersion in water and restriction of the chest wall by strapping, reduces FRC.

11) Formula to calculate minute volume
   a. RR x tidal volume
   b. RR ÷ tidal volume
   c. FiO_2/PEEP
   d. FiO_2/PEEP x RR

Ans: (a)

Total pulmonary ventilation or respiratory minute volume is the amount of air inspired or expired per minute. It is normally about 6 L (i.e., tidal volume of 500 ml X respiratory rate of 12 per minute).

12) In comparison to obstructive lung disease, restrictive lung disease shows decrease of: (Multiple correct answers)
   a. FEVI
   b. Forced residual capacity (FRC)
   c. FEV1/FVC
   d. Total lung capacity (TLC)
   e. Residual volume

Ans: (b, d & e)

The two major types of ventilatory dysfunction are restrictive and obstructive diseases.

Obstructive lung diseases

---

1. Asthma
2. Acute and chronic bronchitis
3. Emphysema
4. Bronchiectasis

5. Cystic fibrosis
6. Bronchiolitis.

In the obstructive pattern, the hallmark is the decreased FEV1/FVC ratio. In obstructive disease, the TLC is normal or increased. RV is usually increased. VC is frequently decreased in obstructive disease because of the elevations in RV with only minor changes in TLC.

The typical feature of restrictive lung diseases is a reduction in the FVC with a normal or elevated FEV1-to-FVC ratio. In restrictive lung diseases (e.g., interstitial fibrosis), the TLC and VC are decreased. Therefore, more than 80% of the FVC can be expelled in the first second accounting for the elevated FEV1-to-FVC ratio.

Restrictive lung diseases (reduction of lung volumes)

---

1. Interstitial lung diseases
2. Pneumonia
3. Disorders of the chest wall or the pleura, which mechanically compress the lungs or limit their expansion
4. Neuromuscular disorders, which decrease the ability of the respiratory muscles to inflate and deflate the lungs

13) Pulmonary function test in restrictive lung disease
    a. Decreased forced vital capacity
    b. Increased forced mid expiratory flow rate
    c. Increased functional residual capacity
    d. Reduced FEV1/FVC

Ans: (a)

FVC (forced vital capacity) is the maximum volume exhaled after a full inspiration, i.e., IRV + TV + ERV. FEV1 is the volume exhaled during the first second of expiration. Normal FEV1 / FVC is 0.75 to 0.80 (75% to

80%). This means that 80% of the FVC can be expelled in the first second itself.

The two major types of ventilatory dysfunction are restrictive and obstructive diseases. Obstructive diseases are asthma, COPD, bronchiectasis, cystic fibrosis, and bronchiolitis. In the obstructive pattern, the hallmark is the decreased FEV1/FVC ratio. In restrictive lung diseases (e.g., interstitial fibrosis), the hallmark is a decrease in lung volumes (TLC and VC). Therefore, more than 80% of the FVC can be expelled in the first second. FEV1 / FVC is normal or increased. In the restrictive pattern, the hallmark is the normal or increased FEV1/FVC ratio.

14) False regarding restrictive lung disease
   a. FEV1/FVC decreased
   b. FVC decreased
   c. TLC decreased
   d. FEV1 increased

   Ans: (a)

FVC (forced vital capacity) is the maximum volume exhaled after a full inspiration, i.e., IRV + TV + ERV. FEV_1 is the volume exhaled during the first second of expiration. Normal FEV_1 / FVC is 0.75 to 0.80 (75% to 80%). This means that 80% of the FVC can be expelled in the first second itself. FEV1/FVC ratio less than 0.7 indicates airflow limitation. Normal or increased FEV1/FVC ratio is typical of restrictive lung disease.

The two major types of ventilatory dysfunction are restrictive and obstructive diseases. Obstructive diseases are asthma, COPD, bronchiectasis, cystic fibrosis, and bronchiolitis. In the obstructive pattern, the hallmark is the decreased FEV1/FVC ratio. In obstructive disease, the *TLC is normal or increased. RV is usually increased.* VC is frequently decreased in obstructive disease because of the elevations in RV with only minor changes in TLC.

17

In restrictive lung diseases (e.g., interstitial fibrosis), the hallmark is a decrease in lung volumes (TLC and VC). Therefore, more than 80% of the FVC can be expelled in the first second. FEV1 / FVC is normal or increased.

15) Which is best to distinguish narrowing of large airway from narrowing of small airways?
   a. Peak expiratory flow rate
   b. Flow-volume loops
   c. Forced expiratory volume in one second
   d. Flow-time loops

Ans: (b)

Flow-volume loop

Upper airway obstruction (UAO) refers to the obstruction of flow in the portion of the airway that extends from the mouth through the length of the trachea and therefore also includes the nasopharynx and larynx. Airflow obstruction due to asthma, COPD and bronchiectasis involves the smaller bronchi in the lower airway distal to the mainstem bronchi.

Forced expiratory volume in one second (FEV1) and forced vital capacity (FVC) are the most readily available and most useful pulmonary function test. The flow-volume loop is a plot of expiratory and inspiratory flow (on the Y-axis) against volume (on the X-axis) during the performance of maximal forced expiratory and inspiratory maneuvers between total lung capacity and residual volume. The contour of the flow-volume loop provides additional information about the location of airway constriction.

The contour of the flow-volume loop is particularly useful for defining whether an obstructing lesion of the upper airway is intrathoracic or extrathoracic and also whether it is fixed (eg, tracheal stenosis, goiter, tumor) or dynamic (eg, structural and functional vocal cord abnormalities, laryngomalacia, extrathoracic tracheomalacia).

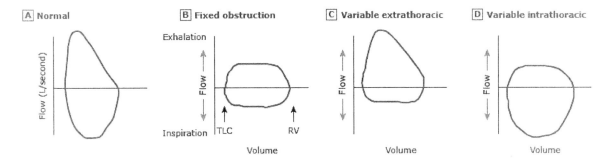

(A) Normal flow-volume loop: the expiratory portion of the flow-volume curve is characterized by a rapid rise to the peak flow rate, followed by a nearly linear fall in flow. The inspiratory curve is a relatively symmetrical, saddle-shaped curve.
(B) Fixed upper airway obstruction (can be intrathoracic or extrathoracic): flow limitation and flattening are noted in both the inspiratory and expiratory limbs of the flow-volume loop.
(C) Dynamic (or variable, nonfixed) extrathoracic obstruction: with flow limitation and flattening are noted on the inspiratory limb of the loop.
(D) Dynamic (or variable, nonfixed) intrathoracic obstruction: flow limitation and flattening are noted on the expiratory limb of the loop.

The flow-volume loop is an insensitive test for upper airway obstruction, as lesions must narrow the tracheal lumen to less than 8 mm (a reduction of the tracheal area by at least 80 percent) before abnormalities can be detected. In general, abnormalities of the upper airway need radiographic and/or direct visualization for confirmation.

16) Normally A-a gradient
   a. 30 mmHg
   b. 20 mmHg
   c. 10 mmHg
   d. 3 mmHg

Ans: (b)

The arterial PO2 is normally a few mm Hg less than the alveolar PO2. The A-a gradient is the difference between the oxygen in the alveoli (PAO2) and the oxygen dissolved in the blood (PaO2). This normal alveolar-arterial oxygen difference is caused mainly by some degree of ventilation-perfusion mismatch and the normal anatomic shunt.

19

The alveolar-arterial PO2 difference is normally about 5 to 15 mm Hg in a young healthy person breathing room air at sea level. It increases with age because of the progressive decrease in arterial PO2 that occurs with aging. The normal alveolar-arterial PO2 difference increases by about 20 mm Hg between the ages of 20 and 70.

The alveolar-arterial oxygen gradient (A-a gradient) is used primarily to differentiate between hypoxia due to hypoventilation (in which the A-a gradient is normal) and hypoxia due to ventilation-perfusion mismatch (in which the A-a gradient is abnormal).

17) Normal mixed venous oxygen tension in an adult after breathing 100% oxygen for 10 minutes
    a. 40 mmHg
    b. 150 mmHg
    c. 740 mmHg
    d. 573 mmHg

Ans: (a)

Normal mixed venous O2 tension (PvO2) is about 40 mm Hg and the normal saturation (Svo2) is about 70%. Mixed venous O2 tension represents the overall balance between O2 consumption and O2 delivery. A true mixed venous blood sample contains venous drainage from the superior vena cava, the inferior vena cava, and the heart; it must therefore be obtained from a pulmonary artery catheter. Mixed venous oxygen saturation provides one of the most important assessments of tissue oxygen metabolism. PvO2 has no practical value at this time.

4 factors determine PvO2. They can be remembered by the mnemonic COAL and include:
- Cardiac output
- Oxygen consumption
- Amount of hemoglobin
- Saturation of Hb

100% oxygen for 10 min does not change the arterial or venous O2 content much. A normal adult will still have a Svo2 around 70-75, or an PvO2 around 40-45.

18) The difference between alveolar partial pressure and arterial partial pressure of oxygen is maximum in
   a. Interstitial lung disease
   b. Acute severe asthma
   c. Pulmonary embolism
   d. Upper airway obstruction due to foreign body

   Ans: (c)

A-a gradient

The Alveolar–arterial gradient (A-a O2 gradient) is a measure of the difference between the alveolar concentration (A) of oxygen and the arterial (a) concentration of oxygen (capital 'A' denotes alveolar and small 'a' denotes arterial). Normal Alveolar-arterial gradient (A-a gradient) is 5 to 10 mmHg. The arterial PO2 (PaO2) is normally a few mm Hg less than the alveolar PO2 (PAO2). This normal alveolar-arterial oxygen difference is caused by the normal anatomic shunt, some degree of ventilation-perfusion mismatch, and diffusion limitation in some parts of the lung. Of these, ventilation-perfusion mismatch is the most important, with a small contribution from shunts and very little from diffusion limitation.

A-a gradient is used to assess the integrity of the alveolar-capillary unit and help determine the cause of low PaO2. A-a gradient of 13 means that if the Alveolar O2 pressure is 100 mm Hg, then the arterial O2 pressure should be above 87 mm Hg. An arterial O2 pressure less than 87 mm Hg would indicate that there is a problem with the transfer of oxygen across the alveolar-capillary unit. *An abnormally increased A-a gradient suggests a defect in V/Q mismatch, right-to-left shunt or a defect in diffusion.*

21

In conditions of high altitude or hypoventilation in which the lung parenchyma is normal, the A-a gradient should be within normal limits. PaO2 is low but only because PAO2 is low. However, transfer of gas from "A" to "a" (A, alveolar; a, arterial) is normal. In contrast, in persons with ventilation-perfusion mismatch, right-to-left shunting or diffusion defects, oxygen is not effectively transferred from the alveoli to the blood and this results in an elevated A-a gradient.

The alveolar-arterial oxygen gradient (A-a gradient) is used primarily to differentiate between hypoxia due to hypoventilation (in which the A-a gradient is normal) and hypoxia due to ventilation-perfusion mismatch (in which the A-a gradient is abnormal).

Upper airway obstruction due to foreign body is an example of a defect in ventilation. It causes low PAO_2 and low PaO_2 and hence, the alveolar arterial oxygen gradient is normal.

19) Compliance curve of the lung is shown below. What does curve marked by arrow mean?

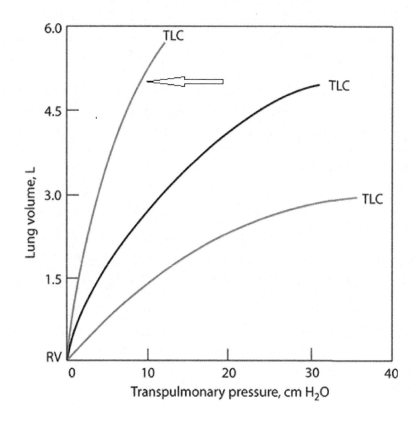

a. Pulmonary fibrosis
b. Atelectasis
c. Emphysema
d. ARDS

Ans: (c)

Lung Compliance

Compliance is a measure of the lung's ability to stretch and expand (distensibility of elastic tissue). Compliance is defined as the change in lung volume (V) as a function of change in pressure (P). Pulmonary compliance is calculated using the equation below:

$C = \Delta V / \Delta P$

C = compliance in L/cm H2O.

ΔV = the change in volume in liters.

ΔP = the change in pressure in cm H2O

Total compliance of the lung and the chest wall is 200 ml/ cm H2O. Low compliance indicates a stiff lung and means extra work is required to bring in a normal volume of air.

Fibrosis will make the lungs less compliant and shift the curve to the right (i.e., for any increase in transpulmonary pressure there is less of an increase in lung volume). The compliance of the chest wall is decreased in obese people, for whom moving the diaphragm downward and the rib cage up and out is much more difficult.

Emphysema increases the compliance of the lungs because it destroys the alveolar septal tissue that normally opposes lung expansion. They have extreme difficulty exhaling air and extra work is required to get air out of the lungs.

Surfactant helps in reducing surface tension and thereby increases compliance of the lung. An absence of the surfactant (Newborn respiratory distress syndrome) leads to a decrease in pulmonary compliance.

In atelectasis, pulmonary compliance decreases due to a decrease in the volume of the lung and requires higher pressure to inflate the alveoli.

Compliance increases with increasing age.

20) Static pulmonary compliance formula:
   a. C = Vt x RR/PEEP
   b. V_t/(plateau pressure – total PEEP
   c. C = Vt/Pplt – PEEP
   d. C = Vt/Pk – Pplt

   Ans: (b)

Both dynamic and static compliance should be calculated. Dynamic compliance is calculated as V_t/(Paw – total PEEP), and plateau or static compliance is V_t/(plateau pressure – total PEEP). Normal values for both dynamic and static compliance are 60 to 100 ml/cm H_2O.

21) Partial pressure of oxygen in aortic blood (PaO2) is not decreased in:
   a. Pulmonary edema
   b. Pulmonary fibrosis
   c. Polycythemia
   d. Cor pulmonale
   e. Pulmonary atelectasis

   Ans: (c)

Partial pressure of oxygen in arterial blood (PaO2) is the blood gas pressure exerted by oxygen dissolved in arterial blood plasma. Arterial Pao2 is the force exerted by dissolved oxygen which acts to keep oxygen on HB. O2 bound to hemoglobin does not contribute to PaO2.

Dissolved O2 is the only form of O2 that produces a partial pressure, which in turn, drives O2 diffusion. PaO2 primarily measures the effectiveness of the lungs in pulling oxygen into the blood stream from the atmosphere.

The normal PaO2 in arterial blood is 95-100 mm Hg. It is reduced in most patients with significant lung disease (eg, asthma, pulmonary edema, obstructive lung disease, interstitial fibrosis, atelectasis.)

Polycythemia and anemia do not affect PaO2. They only affect the oxygen transported by hemoglobin, not the oxygen dissolved in plasma.

22) Diffusion capacity of carbon monoxide is decreased in all except:
   a. Polycythemia
   b. Interstitial lung disease
   c. Emphysema
   d. Pulmonary vascular disease

   Ans: (a)

The diffusing capacity (transfer factor) is a measure of the lung's overall ability to transfer gas into the blood. The ability of gas to diffuse across the alveolar-capillary membrane is assessed by the diffusing capacity of the lung for carbon monoxide (DL CO). The diffusing capacity of the lung for carbon monoxide is the volume of carbon monoxide transferred in milliliters per minute per millimeter of mercury of alveolar partial pressure of CO.

The diffusing capacity of the lungs for carbon monoxide (DLCO) is one of the most valuable tests of lung function. The DLCO is a measure of the ease with which oxygen moves from inhaled air to the red blood cells in the pulmonary capillaries.

The DLCO can be affected by factors that change the membrane properties and also by changes in hemoglobin and capillary blood volume. The normal value of the diffusing capacity for carbon monoxide depends on age, sex, and height (as is the case for most pulmonary function tests).

Obstructive disease

The total volume of blood in the lungs in healthy adults at rest is less than 150 mL. Diseases in which the alveolar-capillary surface area is reduced (eg, idiopathic *pulmonary fibrosis* and *emphysema*) lead to a reduction in the blood volume in the lungs.

The DLCO is an excellent index of the severity of emphysema in smokers with airways obstruction. Smokers with airways obstruction but normal DLCO values usually have chronic "obstructive" bronchitis but not emphysema. Patients with airway obstruction from asthma typically have normal or high DLCO values.

Restrictive disease

The DLCO helps in the differential diagnosis of restrictive lung disease. A low DLCO combined with reduced lung volumes suggests interstitial lung disease. A normal DLCO associated with low volumes is consistent with an extrapulmonary cause of the restriction, such as obesity, pleural effusion or thickening, neuromuscular weakness, or kyphoscoliosis; clinical evaluation and chest imaging are needed for confirmation.

Another common application of the DLCO is for detection of mild (early or preclinical) interstitial lung disease in high-risk patients, including those with:
  ➢ Sarcoidosis
  ➢ Hypersensitivity pneumonitis (extrinsic allergic alveolitis)
  ➢ Chest irradiation and cancer chemotherapy
  ➢ Use of drugs known to have pulmonary toxicity (eg, amiodarone, bleomycin, nitrofurantoin)
  ➢ Rheumatic disease (eg, systemic sclerosis)

Pulmonary vascular disease

An abnormal DLCO may be due to pulmonary vascular disease in those patients with chronic dyspnea but normal spirometry and lung volumes. Reduction in the DLCO is a sensitive indicator of:

- Chronic recurrent pulmonary emboli or chronic thromboembolic pulmonary hypertension
- Idiopathic pulmonary arterial hypertension
- Pulmonary vascular involvement from rheumatic diseases and vasculitides (eg, systemic sclerosis, systemic lupus erythematosus, mixed connective tissue disease)
- Heart failure

In anaemia, the number of red cells in the capillaries is reduced. Then, the rate of combination of carbon monoxide with blood is reduced.

Conditions that decrease the diffusing capacity

Thickening of the barrier
- Interstitial or alveolar edema
- Interstitial or alveolar fibrosis – Sarcoidosis, Scleroderma

Decreased surface area
- Emphysema
- Tumors
- Low cardiac output
- Low pulmonary capillary blood volume

Decreased uptake by erythrocytes
- Anemia
- Low pulmonary capillary blood volume

Ventilation-perfusion mismatch

23) Polysomnography does not include:
   a. Electroencephalography
   b. Pulse oximetry
   c. Electrooculography
   d. Arterial pCO_2 measurement

Ans: (d)

Polysomnography is a diagnostic test for sleep disorders (eg, obstructive sleep apnea syndrome). During PSG, the patient sleeps while connected to a variety of monitoring devices that record physiologic variables.

Measured variables

Assessment of sleep stages requires 3 studies: electroencephalography (EEG), electrooculography (EOG), and surface electromyography (EMG).

Measurement of the following physiologic variables is required during polysomnography.

> Sleep stages —EEG, electrooculogram (EOG), and submental electromyographic activity (EMG) are used to identify the stages of sleep. The submental EMG detects hypotonia, which is typical of REM sleep, and is helpful in detecting involuntary clenching or grinding of the teeth.
> Airflow — Nasal prongs measuring nasal pressure detect inspiratory and expiratory flow and may be the most accurate method to identify subtle inspiratory flow limitation. Nasal pressure is especially helpful in detecting hypopneas.
> Snoring — Snoring is detected with a microphone attached to the neck.
> End-tidal carbon dioxide (CO_2) — An end-tidal carbon dioxide (CO_2) monitor is used to identify hypoventilation in selected studies. This is more commonly used in pediatric studies.
> Oxygen saturation — Pulse oximetry is used to monitor the oxyhemoglobin saturation during PSG.
> Electrocardiogram — Electrocardiography is performed to detect arrhythmias during sleep. A single modified lead II alone is preferred.
> Body position — Some patients only have abnormalities when sleeping in certain positions. Therefore, body position (eg, supine, left lateral, right lateral, prone) is monitored throughout the test using a position sensor and/or video monitor.
> Limb movements — An EMG of the anterior tibialis of both legs is generally monitored during PSG, in order to detect leg movements.
> Video-monitoring using an infrared sensor and a two-way communication system between the sleep study bedroom and

the technologist control room is also important for patient monitoring.

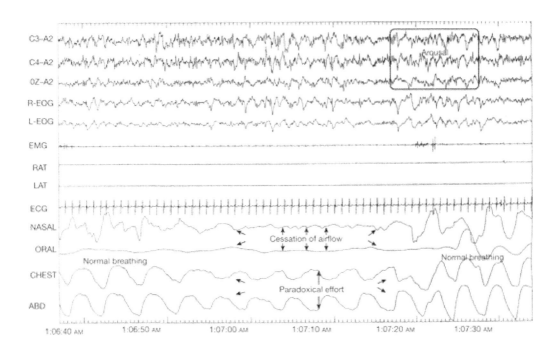

The polysomnography traces from the top down are as follows: Three EEG channels (C3–A2, C4–A2, OZ–A2); two EOG channels (R and L); submental electromyogram (EMG); right and left anterior tibialis EMG (RAT, LAT), electrocardiogram (ECG); nasal and oral airflow; chest and abdominal motion (chest & abd). During the apneic episodes, there is abnormal airflow (both oral and nasal) with paradoxical motion of the rib cage and abdomen. At the end of the apneic episode there is a burst of EMG activity at the arousal. Following the arousal, respiration resumes with synchronous movements of the rib cage and abdomen.

Asthma and allergic diseases

24) Which of the following indicates positive bronchodilator reversibility test in suspected asthma?
   a. Increase in FEV1 > 5% after SABA inhalation
   b. Increase in FEV1 > 12% after SABA inhalation
   c. Increase in FEV1 > 25% after SABA inhalation

29

d. Increase in FEV1 > 50% after SABA inhalation

Ans: (b)

Spirometry measures the forced vital capacity (the maximal amount of air expired from the point of maximal inhalation), and the forced expiratory volume in one second (FEV1). A reduced ratio of FEV1 to FVC indicates airway obstruction. Reversibility is demonstrated by an increase of 12% and 200 mL after the administration of a short-acting bronchodilator.

Albuterol or an equivalent short-acting beta agonist is administered by metered dose inhaler with a spacer or chamber device. Spirometry should be repeated 10 to 15 minutes after administration of a bronchodilator. In a patient with airway obstruction, an increase in the FEV1 of more than 12 percent and greater than 0.2 L suggests acute bronchodilator responsiveness (bronchial asthma).

25) Drugs used in acute asthma: (Multiple correct answers)
   a. Budesonide
   b. Terbutaline
   c. Salbutamol
   d. Theophylline
   e. Sodium cromoglycate

Ans: (b, c)

Severe asthma exacerbation in adults

Standard treatments

> Inhaled beta agonist: salbutamol (albuterol) - The mainstay of treatment are high doses of SABA (short acting beta agonists) given either by nebulizer or via MDI with a spacer. In severely ill patients with impending respiratory failure, IV β2-agonists may be given.
> Oxygen: give sufficient oxygen to maintain SpO2 ≥90 percent (>95 percent in pregnancy)
> IV access: may give normal saline for repletion, if patient is dehydrated due to reduced intake and prolonged episode

- Ipratropium bromide by nebulization - A nebulized anticholinergic may be added if there is not a satisfactory response to β2-agonists alone, as there are additive effects.
- Systemic glucocorticoids: for patients with impending respiratory failure, give methylprednisolone 60 to 125 mg IV. For the majority of less severe asthma exacerbations, give prednisone 40 to 60 mg orally
- Magnesium sulfate: give 2 g IV over 20 minutes for life-threatening exacerbations and exacerbations that remain severe after one hour of intensive bronchodilator therapy

Potential additional treatments
- Epinephrine: for patients suspected of having an anaphylactic reaction or unable to use inhaled bronchodilators for severe asthma exacerbation, give epinephrine 0.3 to 0.5 mg IM; if severe asthma but no evidence of anaphylaxis, can give epinephrine 0.3 to 0.5 mg SC; give epinephrine OR terbutaline but not both
- Terbutaline: may give 0.25 mg by SC injection for severe asthma unresponsive to standard therapies; give terbutaline OR epinephrine but not both

Endotracheal intubation and ventilation
- The decision to intubate during the first few minutes of a severe asthma attack is clinical. *Slowing of the respiratory rate, depressed mental status, inability to maintain respiratory effort, or severe hypoxemia suggests the patient requires intubation.* In the absence of anticipated intubation difficulty, rapid sequence intubation is preferred. Nasal intubation is not recommended.
- The goal of mechanical ventilation is to maintain adequate oxygenation and ventilation while minimizing elevations in airway pressures. This is accomplished by using low tidal volumes (6 to 8 mL/kg), and low respiratory rates (10 to 12/minute). In some patients, elevations in $PaCO_2$ must be tolerated to avoid barotrauma (ie, permissive hypercapnia).

Methylxanthines

The use of intravenous methylxanthines (eg, theophylline, aminophylline) was once the standard of care for severe asthmatic attacks; they have been shown to be relatively ineffective and is no longer recommended in this setting. These agents are not as potent as the beta agonists and do not cause further bronchodilation. In addition, methylxanthines increase the incidence of adverse effects when combined with beta-agonist bronchodilators.

For patients who are taking oral theophylline at presentation, continue maintenance oral therapy (and check a theophylline blood level) during hospitalization.

26) Metered dose inhalers are used in management of asthma. To use a MDI, it is recommended to shake well before use, breathe out, bring the inhaler to your mouth, start to breathe in slowly, press the top of you inhaler once and keep breathing in slowly, until you have taken a full breath and then hold your breath for 10 seconds. Some patients might need a second puff of MDI for symptomatic relief. Which instruction for re-using the MDI is false?
   a. Wait for 1 minute between two puffs
   b. Shake the inhaler again before use
   c. Carefully rinse your mouth and throat
   d. Clean the inhaler before use

Ans: (d)

Inhaler devices are the major method for delivery of asthma medication, but their effectiveness can be compromised if the patient uses the inhaler device incorrectly. Metered dose inhalers (MDI) consist of a pressurized canister, a metering valve and stem, and a mouthpiece actuator. See figure below.

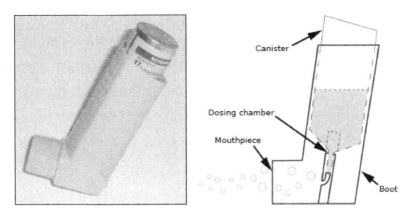

A metered dose inhaler (MDI) is a handheld aerosol device that can deliver the drug directly to the lungs. MDIs include a pressurized metal canister that contains the drug. The canister is housed in a plastic sleeve that has a mouthpiece for drug delivery.

Each inhaler has its own directions. In general, to use a metered dose inhaler, you:

- Take the cap off the mouthpiece.
- Shake the inhaler for 5 seconds.
- Hold the inhaler upright with your finger on the top of the canister and your thumb holding the bottom of the inhaler.
- Breathe out a normal breath.
- Close your lips around the mouthpiece or hold the mouthpiece 1 to 2 inches (4 cm) in front of your mouth.
- As you start to inhale the next breath, press down on the canister.
- Keep inhaling deeply and slowly through your mouth.
- When your lungs are full, hold your breath for 5 to 10 seconds to keep the medicine in your lungs.
- Let your breath out.
- If you are supposed to take 2 puffs of your inhaler, wait 15 to 30 seconds before you take the second puff. Shake the inhaler again before the second puff.
- Put the cap back on the mouthpiece.
- If you use a steroid inhaler, rinse your mouth out with water, gargle, and spit out the water.

MDIs tend to spray out medication more quickly than the patient can inhale. In addition, some patients do not inhale long enough after actuation of the device. As a result, a substantial amount of the medication is deposited in the back of the throat or on the tongue. Oropharyngeal deposition results in inefficient medication delivery and, with inhaled glucocorticoids, may cause hoarseness and thrush.

Cleaning the inhaler

If you use your inhaler every day, clean it at least once a week. If you do not use your inhaler every day, you can clean it less often. To know when you need to clean it, look inside the mouthpiece. Clean your inhaler when you see powder in or around the hole.

27) Adverse effects of salbutamol include all the following, except:
   a. Tremors
   b. Nervousness
   c. Palpitation
   d. Hypoglycemia

Ans: (d)

Unwanted effects are dose related and due to stimulation of extrapulmonary β receptors. Side effects are not common with inhaled therapy but quite common with oral or intravenous administration.

Muscle tremor due to stimulation of β2 receptors in skeletal muscle is the most common side effect.

Tachycardia and palpitations are due to reflex cardiac stimulation secondary to peripheral vasodilation, from direct stimulation of atrial β2 receptors (human heart has a relatively high proportion of β2 receptors), and also from stimulation of myocardial β1 receptors as the doses of β2 agonist are increased.

Hypokalemia is a potentially serious side effect. This is due to β2 receptor stimulation of potassium entry into skeletal muscle, which may be secondary to a rise in insulin secretion. Hypokalemia might be serious in the presence of hypoxia, as in acute asthma, when there may be a predisposition to cardiac arrhythmias. In practice, however, significant arrhythmias after nebulized β2 agonists are rarely observed in acute asthma or patients with COPD.

Ventilation-perfusion V/Q mismatch due to pulmonary vasodilation in blood vessels previously constricted by hypoxia results in the shunting of blood to poorly ventilated areas and a fall in arterial oxygen tension. Although in practice the effect of β2 agonists on PaO2 is usually exceedingly small (<5 mm Hg fall), occasionally in severe COPD it can be large, although it may be prevented by giving additional inspired oxygen.

Metabolic effects (increase in free fatty acid, insulin, glucose, pyruvate, and lactate) are usually seen only after large systemic doses.

Side Effects of β2 Agonists

- Muscle tremor (direct effect on skeletal muscle β2 receptors)
- Tachycardia (direct effect on atrial β2 receptors, reflex effect from increased peripheral vasodilation via β2 receptors)
- Hypokalemia (direct β2 effect on skeletal muscle uptake of K+)
- Restlessness
- Hypoxemia (↑ V/Q mismatch due to reversal of hypoxic pulmonary vasoconstriction)
- Metabolic effects (Increased FFA, glucose, lactate, pyruvate, insulin)

28) All are side effects of salbutamol except
    a. Hypokalemia
    b. Decrease in free fatty acid
    c. Tremor
    d. Tachycardia

Ans: (b)

Unwanted effects of salbutamol are dose related and due to stimulation of extrapulmonary β receptors. Side effects are not common with inhaled therapy but quite common with oral or intravenous administration.

Side Effects of β₂ Agonists

- Muscle tremor (direct effect on skeletal muscle β_2 receptors)
- Tachycardia (direct effect on atrial β_2 receptors, reflex effect from increased peripheral vasodilation via β_2 receptors)
- Hypokalemia (direct β_2 effect on skeletal muscle uptake of K^+)
- Restlessness
- Hypoxemia ($\uparrow$ V̇/Q̇ mismatch due to reversal of hypoxic pulmonary vasoconstriction)
- Metabolic effects ($\uparrow$ FFA, glucose, lactate, pyruvate, insulin)

29) All adverse effects of theophylline mediated by A1 receptor except:
   a. Cardiac arrhythmias
   b. Diuresis
   c. Seizures
   d. Hyperkalemia

   Ans: (d)

Oral theophylline is a fourth-line agent for treating COPD patients who do not achieve adequate symptom control with inhaled anticholinergic, beta-2-agonist, and corticosteroid therapies. Sustained-release theophylline improves hemoglobin saturation during sleep in COPD patients and is a first-line agent for those with sleep-related breathing disorders. Theophylline improves dyspnea ratings, exercise performance, and pulmonary function in many patients with stable COPD. Its benefits result from bronchodilation; anti-inflammatory properties; and extrapulmonary effects on diaphragm strength, myocardial contractility, and kidney function.

Theophylline toxicity is a significant concern due to the medication's narrow therapeutic window, and long-term administration requires careful monitoring of serum levels.

Adverse events observed at therapeutic serum levels.

➢ Cardiovascular: Cardiac flutter, tachycardia
➢ Central nervous system: Headache, hyperactivity (children), insomnia, restlessness, seizure, status epilepticus (nonconvulsive)
➢ Endocrine & metabolic: Hypercalcemia (with concomitant hyperthyroid disease), hyperglycemia, and hypokalemia
➢ Gastrointestinal: Gastroesophageal reflux (aggravation), gastrointestinal ulcer (aggravation), nausea, vomiting
➢ Genitourinary: Difficulty in micturition (elderly males with prostatism), diuresis (transient)
➢ Neuromuscular & skeletal: Tremor

30) A 50-year-old presents with acute exacerbation of asthma. He complains of nocturnal cough, limitation of daily activities in spite of good compliance with medications. He has been having severe persistent asthma in the last 14 years of age. The disease was well controlled till last year with high dose inhaled corticosteroids. However, the same dose has not given relief for the last 1 year. Spirometry is suggestive of bronchial asthma with partial irreversibility of airway obstruction. What is the cause for poor disease control?
   a. Airway epithelial shedding
   b. Airway inflammation
   c. Airway remodeling
   d. Airway hyper-responsiveness

Ans: (c)

Asthma is a chronic inflammatory airway disorder characterized by airway hyperresponsiveness and reversible airflow obstruction. Subgroups of asthma patients develop airflow obstruction that is irreversible or only partially reversible and experience an accelerated rate of lung function decline. The structural changes in the airways of these patients are referred to as airway remodeling. In asthma, irreversible structural changes in the airway walls are characterized by the following:

- Epithelial damage
- Collagen deposition in sub-epithelial reticular basement membrane
- Smooth muscle hyperplasia and hypertrophy/ increased smooth muscle mass
- Destruction of elastic tissue
- Mucus gland hypertrophy
- Angiogenesis

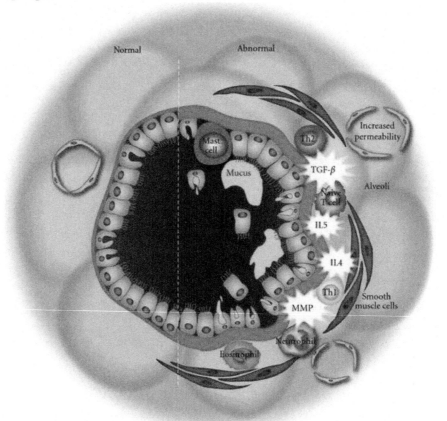

Airway remodeling (abnormal half of figure) involves almost all elements of the airway wall and occurs throughout the bronchial tree.

These remodeling changes contribute to thickening of airway walls and consequently lead to airway narrowing, bronchial hyperresponsiveness, airway edema, and mucous hypersecretion. Airway remodeling is associated with poorer clinical outcome among patients with asthma.

31) True about tropical pulmonary eosinophilia
    a. Total serum IgE levels are markedly elevated
    b. It affects males more than females
    c. Develops in individuals with filariasis
    d. All the above

Ans: (d)

Pulmonary filariasis (Tropical pulmonary eosinophilia)

Infection with W. bancrofti or B. malayi cause tropical pulmonary eosinophilia. Only a small number of individuals are susceptible to tropical pulmonary eosinophilia. Patients with tropical pulmonary eosinophilia have marked immune responses to filariae.

Patients with pulmonary filariasis show humoral hyperreactivity manifested as increased serum levels of total IgE and antifilarial IgG and IgE. These antibodies cause rapid clearance of microfilariae. In tropical pulmonary eosinophilia, there are high concentrations of antifilarial IgG and IgE in serum and bronchoalveolar lavage (BAL) fluid, but blood examinations for parasites are invariably negative.

Young males are predominantly afflicted by tropical pulmonary eosinophilia. The syndrome is characterized by episodes of dry night cough, low-grade fever, and general fatigue. Examination of the chest may reveal coarse crackles and rhonchi, along with wheezing. Clinically, it may be mistaken for asthma.

Eosinophil counts in peripheral blood generally exceed 3000/mm3. Radiographically, the syndrome may be associated with reticulonodular opacities and increased bronchovascular markings.

32) True about hypersensitivity pneumonitis: (Multiple correct answers)
   a. May occur due to inorganic antigens
   b. Increased CD8+ T cells in bronchoalveolar lavage
   c. Manifests mainly as an occupational and environment disease
   d. For severe acute cases, oral steroids are given for 3-4 weeks
   e. Interstitial infiltrate is seen in chest x-ray

Ans: (a, b, c, d, e)

Hypersensitivity pneumonitis, or extrinsic allergic alveolitis, is an inflammatory syndrome of the lung caused by inhalation of antigenic agents in a susceptible host.

Numerous organic and inorganic antigens can cause hypersensitivity pneumonitis. The main difference between organic and inorganic compounds is that organic compounds contain carbon-hydrogen bonds, while inorganic compounds do not contain either of those two atoms. Organic compounds are generally found in living matter and include nucleic acids, lipids and fatty acids, proteins and enzymes, and more. Inorganic compounds are generally obtained from non-living matter and include the salts, metals, and other elemental compounds.

The antigens responsible for hypersensitivity pneumonitis are classified into three major categories: microbes (farmer's lung), animal proteins (bird fancier's lung), and low-molecular-weight chemicals (chemical worker's lung).

Hypersensitivity pneumonitis results from a type III (immune-complex mediated) or type IV (T-cell mediated) hypersensitivity response.

BAL is the most sensitive tool to detect an alveolitis in patients suspected of having HP. BAL typically shows a marked increase in lymphocytes and a predominance of CD8-positive T lymphocytes over CD4-positive T lymphocytes. This is a reversal of the normal CD4:CD8 ratio, in which CD4-positive cells predominate. *The BAL CD4+/CD8+ ratio is usually decreased to less than 1* (normal ratio = 2.3 ± 0.2).

A marked BAL lymphocytosis (greater than 20 percent and often exceeding 50 percent of the white blood cells recovered) is a nonspecific but helpful finding; this level of lymphocytosis is uncommon in diseases generally considered in the differential diagnosis.

BAL neutrophils may be elevated to more than 5 percent of white cells after recent antigen exposure, or in advanced disease.

The finding of substantial numbers of mast cells (greater than 1 percent of recovered white cells), especially if associated with a marked BAL lymphocytosis, may be specific for HP. Mast cells are usually increased following acute exposure and decline toward normal within one to three months.

Occupational and environment disease

Hypersensitivity pneumonitis is caused by an inappropriate inflammatory response to an environmental exposure. A wide range of occupations that result in contact with airborne organic antigens increase the risk of developing HP. Common occupations associated with HP include farming (farmer's lung), chemical manufacturing and bird breeding (bird fancier's lung). Farmer's lung is one of the most common forms of HP, affecting the farming population. The key to treatment is identifying the causative agent and eliminating continued exposure.

Disease	Antigen	Source
Farmer's lung	*Micropolyspora faeni, Thermoactinomyces vulgaris*	Moldy hay
"Humidifier" lung	Thermophilic actinomycetes	Contaminated humidifiers, heating systems, or air conditioners
Bird fancier's lung ("pigeon-breeder's disease")	Avian proteins	Bird serum and excreta
Bagassosis	*Thermoactinomyces sacchari* and *T vulgaris*	Moldy sugar cane fiber (bagasse)
Sequoiosis	Graphium, Aureobasidium, and other fungi	Moldy redwood sawdust
Maple bark stripper's disease	*Cryptostroma (Coniosporium) corticale*	Rotting maple tree logs or bark
Mushroom picker's disease	Same as farmer's lung	Moldy compost
Suberosis	*Penicillium frequentans*	Moldy cork dust
Detergent worker's lung	*Bacillus subtilis* enzyme	Enzyme additives

Chest radiography

In acute hypersensitivity pneumonitis, a poorly defined micronodular or diffuse interstitial pattern is typical.

Treatment of acute hypersensitivity pneumonitis consists of identification of the offending agent and avoidance of further exposure. In severe acute or protracted cases, oral corticosteroids (prednisone, 0.5 mg/kg daily as a single morning dose for 2 weeks, tapered to nil over 4–6 weeks) may be given.

Rituximab, a B cell depleting monoclonal antibody, has been used in individual cases of refractory hypersensitivity pneumonitis.

33) A patient presents with cough with expectoration. True statement regarding acute farmers lung:
   a. Type III hypersensitivity reaction
   b. Persistent cough with expectoration
   c. Eosinophilia
   d. X-ray shows predominant upper lobe lesions

   Ans: (c)

Farmer's lung results from inhalational exposure to thermophilic Actinomyces species and occasionally from exposure to various Aspergillus species. Exposure to large quantities of contaminated hay is the most common inhalational source.

Both humoral and cell-mediated immune responses play a role in pathogenesis. There is involvement of immune complex–induced tissue injury (type III hypersensitivity). Cell-mediated, delayed-type hypersensitivity (type IV hypersensitivity) also plays a major role in the pathogenesis of this syndrome.

Acute farmer's lung manifests as new onset of fever, nonproductive cough, dyspnea, headache, and malaise. If the inhalational exposure is large, patients may develop acute respiratory failure.

In acute farmer's lung, physical findings are as follows:
- Fever
- Tachycardia

- Nonproductive cough
- Rales that persist after fever subsides
- Wheezing (rare)

Leukocytosis with neutrophilia (but not eosinophilia) and elevated erythrocyte sedimentation rate (ESR) are noted.

Diffuse air-space consolidation is typical of acute farmer's lung (with acute antigen exposure).

Pulmonary apices are often spared on plain chest radiography.

34) A 28-year-old man presents with cough, shortness of breath and wheezing. Initially these symptoms developed only when he was running; but recently the symptoms are present while walking and sometimes even at rest. He had atopic dermatitis in childhood. His father and sister also had atopic dermatitis. He also has hay fever from 14 years of age. What is the cause of bronchospasm?
   a. COPD
   b. Smoking
   c. Type 1 hypersensitivity
   d. Exercise

Ans: (c)

Shortness of breath and wheezing associated with history of atopic dermatitis and hay fever (allergic rhinoconjunctivitis) points to the diagnosis of allergic asthma.

Type I hypersensitivity (immediate hypersensitivity) is a type of immune reaction in which tissue is damaged due to IgE antibody. Most allergies are caused by type I hypersensitivity reactions. Type I reactions (ie, immediate hypersensitivity reactions) involve IgE–mediated release of histamine and other mediators from mast cells

44

and basophils. Examples include anaphylaxis, asthma and allergic rhinoconjunctivitis (hay fever).

In allergic asthma, an allergen is initially exposed to dendritic cells functioning as antigen-presenting cells. These cells interact with B lymphocytes to produce immunoglobulin E (IgE) in the context of appropriate cytokine and T lymphocyte interactions. Circulating IgE binds high-affinity receptors in blood and tissue mast cells and low-affinity receptors on the surface of lymphocytes, eosinophils, neutrophils, platelets, and macrophages, thus recruiting these cells to the airways. Subsequent exposures to the same antigen will crossbridge IgE bound to mast cell receptors, facilitating mast cell degranulation and release of various cytokines and chemokines, which recruit additional inflammatory cells to the lungs.

Atopy is the major risk factor for asthma, and nonatopic individuals have a very low risk of developing asthma. Patients with asthma commonly suffer from other atopic diseases, particularly allergic rhinitis (hay fever) and atopic dermatitis (eczema).

35) Not a feature of allergic bronchopulmonary aspergillosis
   a. Recurrent pneumonia
   b. Fungal invasion of the respiratory tract mucosa
   c. Central bronchiectasis
   d. Absence of IgE sensitization to Aspergillus excludes ABPA

Ans: (b)

Allergic bronchopulmonary aspergillosis (ABPA) is a hypersensitivity reaction of the airways that occurs when bronchi become colonized by Aspergillus species. ABPA most commonly develops in patients with asthma but can also develop in patients with cystic fibrosis. Repeated episodes of bronchial obstruction, inflammation, and mucoid impaction can lead to bronchiectasis, fibrosis, and respiratory compromise.

ABPA is characterized pathologically by mucoid impaction of the bronchi, eosinophilic pneumonia, and bronchocentric granulomatosis. Septated hyphae with acute dichotomous branching may be seen in the mucus-filled bronchial lumen, but fungi rarely invade the mucosa. The clinical picture of ABPA is dominated by asthma and recurrent exacerbations. Central bronchiectasis (affects inner one-half to two-thirds of lung) may develop.

Establishing IgE sensitization to Aspergillus through either skin prick test or measurement of specific serum IgE is a reasonable first step in an asthmatic being evaluated for ABPA. Inability to establish IgE sensitization to Aspergillus virtually excludes ABPA from consideration. If skin testing and/or specific IgE are positive, total serum IgE, precipitins to Aspergillus, and eosinophil count should be assayed. Chest imaging, preferably with a chest CT, should be performed as well.

36) Most common cause of Loffler's syndrome
   a. Tape worms
   b. Filariasis
   c. Cysticercosis
   d. Ascaris

Ans: (d)

Transpulmonary passage of helminth larvae (Löffler syndrome)
Löffler syndrome is related to the transit of parasitic organisms through the lungs during their life cycle in the human host. Ascaris is the most common cause of Löffler syndrome worldwide. After ingestion of Ascaris lumbricoides eggs, larvae hatch in the intestine and penetrate the mesenteric lymphatics and venules to enter the pulmonary circulation. They lodge in the pulmonary capillaries and continue the cycle by migrating through the alveolar walls. Finally, they move up the bronchial tree and are swallowed, returning to the intestine, and maturing into adult forms. This process takes approximately 10-16 days after ingestion of the eggs. Other parasites, such as Necator americanus, Ancylostoma duodenale, and

Strongyloides stercoralis, have a similar cycle to Ascaris, with passage of larval forms through the alveolar walls.

Löffler syndrome is a transient respiratory illness associated with blood eosinophilia and radiographic shadowing. Symptoms of Löffler syndrome are usually mild or absent and tend to spontaneously resolve after several days or, at most, after 2-3 weeks. Cough is the most common symptom among symptomatic patients. It is usually dry and unproductive but may be associated with production of small amounts of mucoid sputum. Symptoms appear 10-16 days after ingestion of Ascaris eggs. A similar timeframe has been described for Löffler syndrome associated with N americanus, A duodenale, or S stercoralis infection.

Usually, no abnormalities are found on physical examination. Occasionally, crackles or wheezes may be heard on lung auscultation.

The minimal nature of symptoms in most patients with Löffler syndrome usually denotes that no pharmacologic therapy is required for this self-limiting condition.

37) Drug that can cause pulmonary eosinophilia
   a. Nitrofurantoin
   b. Valproate
   c. Enalapril
   d. Ciprofloxacin

Ans: (a)

NSAIDs and antimicrobials (eg, nitrofurantoin, minocycline, sulfonamides, ampicillin, daptomycin) are the most common classes of drugs associated with pulmonary eosinophilia.

The clinical presentation includes asymptomatic pulmonary infiltration with eosinophilia, chronic cough with or without dyspnea and fever, acute eosinophilic pneumonia, and drug reaction with eosinophilia and systemic symptoms (DRESS). DRESS should be suspected when the patient has a skin eruption, fever, facial edema, enlarged lymph nodes, and a history of initiation of a culprit medication two to six weeks prior to disease onset.

COPD

38) Gold's criteria for severe COPD-
   a. FEV1 /FVC < 0.7; FEV, > 80%
   b. FEV1 / FVC < 0.7; FEV, < 80%
   c. FEV1 / FVC < 0.7; FEV, < 50%
   d. FEV1 / FVC < 0.7; FEV, < 30%

   Ans: (c)

The hallmark of COPD is airflow obstruction. The diagnosis of COPD is made with spirometry; when the ratio of forced expiratory volume in 1 second over forced vital capacity (FEV1/FVC) is less than 70% of that predicted for a matched control. The degree of airflow obstruction is an important prognostic factor in COPD and is the basis for the GOLD spirometric severity classification. Criteria for assessing the severity of airflow obstruction (based on the percent predicted postbronchodilator FEV1) are shown in table below.

GOLD Criteria for Severity of Airflow Obstruction in COPD

GOLD Stage	Severity	Spirometry
I	Mild	FEV_1/FVC <0.7 and FEV_1 ≥80% predicted
II	Moderate	FEV_1/FVC <0.7 and FEV_1 ≥50% but <80% predicted
III	Severe	FEV_1/FVC <0.7 and FEV_1 ≥30% but <50% predicted
IV	Very severe	FEV_1/FVC <0.7 and FEV_1 <30% predicted

39) How does alpha-1 antitrypsin prevent lung tissue destruction?

a. Inhibiting the release of trypsin
b. Inhibiting the activation of trypsinogen
c. Inhibiting the release of chymotrypsin
d. Inhibiting the elastase of neutrophils in lung

Ans: (d)

Alpha-1 antitrypsin (AAT) inhibits the enzyme elastase, which destroys elastin in the lung. AAT protects against degradation of elastin by inhibiting elastase. Cigarette smoking and infection increase the elastase action in the lung, thus increasing lung degradation. Alpha-1 antitrypsin protects the lower airways from damage caused by proteolytic enzymes, such as elastase.

Clinical manifestations of severe deficiency of AAT typically involve the lung (eg, early onset emphysema), liver (eg, cirrhosis), and, rarely, the skin (eg, panniculitis).

40) A 60-year-old man presents with gradually worsening shortness of breath and productive cough that have been present for 15 years. He is a heavy smoker. He has tried nicotine patches and bupropion but is still unable to quit smoking. Physical exam reveals bilateral extensive wheezing. Pulmonary function tests show FEV1/FVC of 55% with no change in FEV1 after albuterol inhalation. What is the most likely underlying pathology?
a. Abnormal permanent bronchial dilation
b. Inflamed bronchus with hypertrophy and hyperplasia of mucous glands
c. Airway hypersensitivity
d. Chronic granulomatous inflammation with bilateral hilar lymphadenopathy

Ans: (b)

Gradually worsening shortness of breath and productive cough in a heavy smoker points to the diagnosis of COPD (chronic obstructive pulmonary disease). FEV1/FVC of 55% with no change in FEV1 after albuterol inhalation indicates irreversible airway obstruction (point against bronchial asthma and airway hypersensitivity).

FVC (forced vital capacity) is the maximum volume exhaled after a full inspiration, i.e., IRV + TV + ERV. FEV_1 is the volume exhaled during the first second of expiration. Normal FEV_1 / FVC is 0.75 to 0.80 (75% to 80%). This means that 80% of the FVC can be expelled in the first second itself.

Most cases of COPD are the result of exposure to noxious stimuli, most often cigarette smoke. Pathologic changes in COPD occur in the large (central) airways, the small (peripheral) bronchioles, and the lung parenchyma. The normal inflammatory response is amplified in persons prone to COPD development.

Mucous gland hyperplasia is the histologic hallmark of chronic bronchitis. Cigarette smoking often results in mucus gland enlargement and goblet cell hyperplasia, leading to cough and mucus production. Goblet cells not only increase in number but in extent through the bronchial tree.

The major site of increased resistance in most individuals with COPD is in airways < 2 mm diameter. Characteristic cellular changes include goblet cell metaplasia, with these mucus-secreting cells replacing surfactant-secreting Clara cells. Smooth-muscle hypertrophy may also be present. These abnormalities may cause luminal narrowing by fibrosis, excess mucus, edema, and cellular infiltration.

Abnormal permanent bronchial dilation indicates bronchiectasis.

Chronic granulomatous inflammation with bilateral hilar lymphadenopathy indicates sarcoidosis.

ARDS

41) ARDS diagnostic criteria
   a. PaO_2/FiO_2 less than 100 mm Hg

b. PaO$_2$/FiO$_2$ less than 200 mm Hg
c. PaO$_2$/FiO$_2$ less than 300 mm Hg
d. PaO$_2$/FiO$_2$ less than 400 mm Hg

Ans: (c)

ARDS can be diagnosed once cardiogenic pulmonary edema and alternative causes of acute hypoxemic respiratory failure and bilateral infiltrates have been excluded. The Berlin Definition of ARDS requires that all the following criteria be present for diagnosis:

➢ Respiratory symptoms must have begun within one week of a known clinical insult, or the patient must have new or worsening symptoms during the past week.

➢ Bilateral opacities must be present on a chest radiograph or CT scan. These opacities must not be fully explained by pleural effusions, lobar collapse, lung collapse, or pulmonary nodules.

➢ The patient's respiratory failure must not be fully explained by cardiac failure or fluid overload. An objective assessment (eg, echocardiography) to exclude hydrostatic pulmonary edema is required if no risk factors for ARDS are present.

➢ A moderate to severe impairment of oxygenation must be present, as defined by the ratio of arterial oxygen tension to fraction of inspired oxygen (PaO2/FiO2). The severity of the hypoxemia defines the severity of the ARDS:

  o Mild ARDS – The PaO2/FiO2 is >200 mmHg, but ≤300 mmHg, on ventilator settings that include positive end-expiratory pressure (PEEP) or continuous positive airway pressure (CPAP) ≥5 cm H2O.

  o Moderate ARDS – The PaO2/FiO2 is >100 mmHg, but ≤200 mmHg, on ventilator settings that include PEEP ≥5 cm H2O.

  o Severe ARDS – The PaO2/FiO2 is ≤100 mmHg on ventilator settings that include PEEP ≥5 cm H2O.

Determining the PaO2/FiO2 requires arterial blood gas (ABG) analysis. For patients in whom an ABG cannot be obtained, the ratio of oxyhemoglobin saturation measured by pulse oximetry (SpO2) to FiO2 may be an appropriate substitute. This approach may be less reliable for patients with mild ARDS.

42) False about ARDS
   a. PaO2 / FiO2 < 200 mmHg
   b. PCWP > 18 mmHg Hg
   c. Onset of illness within one week of a known clinical insult
   d. Bilateral alveolar infiltrates

Ans: (b)

ARDS is characterized clinically by the rapid onset of severe life-threatening respiratory insufficiency (within 24 hours), cyanosis, and severe arterial hypoxemia that is refractory to oxygen therapy. It may progress to multisystem organ failure.

The pulmonary infiltrates are caused by damage to the alveolar capillary membrane.

Pulmonary wedge pressure more than 18mmHg suggests cardiac failure. PCWP should be normal in ARDS. There should not be any evidence of primary left sided heart failure if ARDS is to be diagnosed.

Clinical diagnosis (Berlin definition)
ARDS can be diagnosed once cardiogenic pulmonary edema and alternative causes of acute hypoxemic respiratory failure and bilateral infiltrates have been excluded. The Berlin Definition of ARDS requires that all of the following criteria be present for diagnosis:
   • Respiratory symptoms must have begun within one week of a known clinical insult, or the patient must have new or worsening symptoms during the past week.
   • Bilateral diffuse alveolar opacities must be present on a chest radiograph or CT scan. These opacities must not be fully explained by pleural effusions, lobar collapse, lung collapse, or pulmonary nodules.
   • The patient's respiratory failure must not be fully explained by cardiac failure or fluid overload (PCWP < 18 mmHg Hg.) An

objective assessment (eg, echocardiography) to exclude hydrostatic pulmonary edema is required if no risk factors for ARDS are present.

- A moderate to severe impairment of oxygenation must be present, as defined by the ratio of arterial oxygen tension to fraction of inspired oxygen (PaO2/FiO2). The severity of the hypoxemia defines the severity of the ARDS:
  - Mild ARDS – The PaO2/FiO2 is >200 mmHg, but ≤300 mmHg, on ventilator settings that include positive end-expiratory pressure (PEEP) or continuous positive airway pressure (CPAP) ≥5 cm H2O.
  - Moderate ARDS – The PaO2/FiO2 is >100 mmHg, but ≤200 mmHg, on ventilator settings that include PEEP ≥5 cm H2O.
  - Severe ARDS – The PaO2/FiO2 is ≤100 mmHg on ventilator settings that include PEEP ≥5 cm H2O.

Normal PaO2/FiO2 at sea level is > 500mmHg. PaO2:FiO2 < 300 is consistent with ALI (acute lung injury). PaO2:FiO2 < 200 is consistent with ARDS.

43) Value of PaO2/ FiO2 characteristic of ARDS-
   a. < 300 mmHg
   b. < 200 mmHg
   c. < 100 mmHg
   d. < 50 mmHg

   Ans: (a)

A moderate to severe impairment of oxygenation must be present, as defined by the ratio of arterial oxygen tension to fraction of inspired oxygen (PaO2/FiO2). The severity of the hypoxemia defines the severity of the ARDS:

- Mild ARDS – The PaO2/FiO2 is >200 mmHg, but ≤300 mmHg, on ventilator settings that include positive end-expiratory pressure (PEEP) or continuous positive airway pressure (CPAP) ≥5 cm H2O.

53

- Moderate ARDS – The PaO2/FiO2 is >100 mmHg, but ≤200 mmHg, on ventilator settings that include PEEP ≥5 cm H2O.
- Severe ARDS – The PaO2/FiO2 is ≤100 mmHg on ventilators setting that include PEEP ≥5 cm H2O.

44) Not an evidenced based recommended therapy for acute respiratory distress syndrome
   a. Low tidal volume mechanical ventilation
   b. Inhaled nitric oxide
   c. Minimize left atrial filling pressures
   d. Prone positioning

Ans: (b)

ARDS

Mechanical ventilation

For most patients, the recommendation is to proceed directly to invasive mechanical ventilation, rather than performing an initial trial of noninvasive positive pressure ventilation. Volume limited and pressure limited modes are both acceptable; however, volume limited approaches have been more extensively studied and there is no evidence the pressure limited approaches confer additional benefit.

For all patients, the tidal volume and respiratory rate be managed using the strategy of low tidal volume ventilation (LTVV). After setting the initial tidal volume based on predicted body weight, adjust the tidal volume to achieve an inspiratory plateau airway pressure ≤30 cm H2O.

The routine use of open lung ventilation, high PEEP, and recruitment maneuvers should be avoided.

Fluid management in ARDS

Increased vascular permeability is the primary cause of pulmonary edema in early ARDS. The quantity of edema formed depends directly upon hydrostatic pressure. As a result, pulmonary edema is more likely to develop in ARDS than in normals for any given pulmonary capillary hydrostatic pressure. Thus, even in patients who are not volume overloaded, a strategy of conservative fluid management may help patients by reducing edema formation. Use a conservative strategy of fluid management in patients with ARDS, as long as hypotension and organ hypoperfusion can be avoided (central venous pressure of <4 mmHg or a pulmonary artery occlusion pressure <8 mmHg). A clear benefit of conservative fluid management on mortality has not yet been shown.

Prone positioning

Prone positioning improves oxygenation in most patients with ARDS. Invasive mechanical ventilation is traditionally delivered with the patient in the supine position. Prone ventilation is ventilation that is delivered with the patient lying in the prone position. Prone ventilation may be used for the treatment of ARDS to improve oxygenation when more traditional modes of ventilation fail (eg, lung protective ventilation).

Nitric oxide

Inhaled nitric oxide (NO) has not become routine therapy for adults with ARDS because, although it improves oxygenation modestly, it has not been shown to reduce morbidity or mortality and is associated with a risk of renal impairment. This lack of proven beneficial outcome and potential harm argue against the routine use of inhaled NO in settings other than refractory hypoxemia.

Respiratory failure

45) Which one of the following is an example of Type-IV respiratory failure?
    a. Bronchial asthma
    b. Pulmonary embolism
    c. COPD
    d. Shock

Ans: (d)

Respiratory failure

Respiration primarily occurs at the alveolar capillary units of the lungs, where exchange of oxygen and carbon dioxide between alveolar gas and blood takes place. Respiratory failure is a syndrome in which the respiratory system fails in one or both of its gas exchange functions: oxygenation and carbon dioxide elimination. It may be classified as either hypoxemic or hypercapnic.

Hypoxemic respiratory failure (type I)

Hypoxemic respiratory failure (type I) is characterized by an arterial oxygen tension (PaO_2) lower than 60 mm Hg with a *normal or low $PaCO_2$*. This is the commonest form of respiratory failure. It can be associated with virtually all acute diseases of the lung. Some examples of type I respiratory failure are asthma, cardiogenic or noncardiogenic pulmonary edema (ARDS), pneumonia, and pulmonary hemorrhage.

V/Q mismatch is the most common cause of hypoxemia.

Hypercapnic respiratory failure (type II)

Hypercapnic respiratory failure (type II) is characterized by a *$PaCO_2$ higher than 50 mm Hg*. Hypoxemia is common in patients with hypercapnic respiratory failure who are breathing room air. The pH depends on the level of bicarbonate, which, in turn, is dependent on the duration of hypercapnia. Common etiologies include severe airway disorders (eg, asthma and COPD), drug overdose, neuromuscular disease, and chest wall abnormalities.

Hypercapnic respiratory failure (type II) respiratory failure is a consequence of alveolar hypoventilation and results from the inability to eliminate carbon dioxide effectively.

Perioperative respiratory failure (Type III)

This form of respiratory failure results from lung atelectasis. Because atelectasis occurs so commonly in the perioperative period, this form is also called perioperative respiratory failure.

After general anesthesia, decreases in functional residual capacity lead to collapse of dependent lung units. Such atelectasis can be treated by frequent changes in position, chest physiotherapy, upright positioning, and control of incisional and/or abdominal pain. Noninvasive positive-pressure ventilation may also be used to reverse regional atelectasis.

Type IV respiratory failure

This form results from hypoperfusion of respiratory muscles in patients in shock. Normally, respiratory muscles consume <5% of total cardiac output and oxygen delivery. Patients in shock often experience respiratory distress due to pulmonary edema (e.g., in cardiogenic shock), lactic acidosis, and anemia. In this setting, up to 40% of cardiac output may be distributed to the respiratory muscles. Intubation and mechanical ventilation can allow redistribution of the cardiac output away from the respiratory muscles and back to vital organs while the shock is treated.

46) A 52-year-old obese female came to emergency with breathlessness, cough and orthopnea of 2 days duration. The PR is 96/min, BP is 140/90mmHg and her respiratory rate is 32/min. SP02 is 76%. Blood gas analysis showed P02 – 56 mm Hg, PC02 – 24 mm Hg and pH - 7.48. How would you manage?
   a. Intubation with low tidal volume mechanical ventilation
   b. Continuous positive pressure ventilation
   c. IV diuretics with digoxin
   d. High flow oxygen through non rebreathing face mask

Answer: (d) Diagnosis is type 1 respiratory failure. There is only mild hypoxemia. The hypocapnia and respiratory alkalosis is due to compensatory hyperventilation.

Hypoxemic respiratory failure (type 1) is characterized by an arterial oxygen tension (Pa O2) lower than 60 mm Hg with a normal or low arterial carbon dioxide tension (Pa CO2). This is the most common form of respiratory failure, and it can be associated with almost all acute diseases of the lung. V/Q mismatch is the most common cause of hypoxemia. Some examples of type I respiratory failure are cardiogenic or noncardiogenic pulmonary edema, pneumonia, and pulmonary hemorrhage.

Hypercapnic respiratory failure (type 2) is characterized by a PaCO2 higher than 50 mm Hg. Hypoxemia is common in patients with hypercapnic respiratory failure who are breathing room air. The pH depends on the level of bicarbonate, which, in turn, is dependent on the duration of hypercapnia. Common etiologies include drug overdose, neuromuscular disease, chest wall abnormalities, and severe airway disorders (eg, asthma and COPD).

Hypoxemia is the most life-threatening aspect of acute respiratory failure. The first objective in the management of respiratory failure is to reverse and/or prevent tissue hypoxia. Adequate oxygen delivery to tissues is generally achieved with an arterial oxygen tension (Pa O2) of 60 mm Hg or arterial oxygen saturation (Sa O2) greater than 90%. Supplemental oxygen is administered via nasal prongs or face mask; however, in patients with severe hypoxemia, intubation and mechanical ventilation are often required.

Whether emergency intubation is required depends on the clinical circumstances. In selected patients, use of noninvasive mechanical ventilation may obviate the need for intubation.

Ventilatory support via a nasal or full-face mask rather than via an endotracheal tube is increasingly being employed for patients with acute or chronic respiratory failure. See figure below.

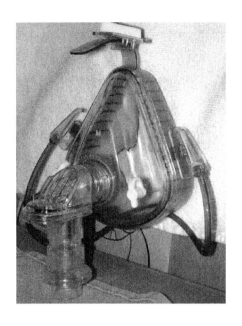

Noninvasive ventilation should be considered in patients with mild-to-moderate acute respiratory failure. The patient should have an intact airway, airway-protective reflexes, and be alert enough to follow commands.

Patients with obesity-hypoventilation syndrome benefit from NPPV (noninvasive positive-pressure ventilation) as a consequence of reversal of the alveolar hypoventilation and upper-airway obstruction.

If an acceptable level of oxygenation, as judged by arterial blood gases, cannot be attained using a face mask, or if administration of supplemental O2 causes hypercapnia to worsen significantly (e.g., in some patients with COPD), mechanical ventilation (invasive or noninvasive) is required.

47) Respiratory failure type II is seen in: (Multiple correct answers)
   a. Myasthenia gravis
   b. Acute exacerbation in COPD
   c. Acute severe asthma
   d. Pulmonary edema
   e. Pulmonary embolism

Ans: (a, b, c)

Respiratory failure is characterized by inadequate blood oxygenation or carbon dioxide removal. Respiratory failure may be classified as either hypoxemic or hypercapnic.

Hypoxemic respiratory failure (type I) is characterized by an arterial oxygen tension (PaO2) lower than 60 mm Hg with a normal or low arterial carbon dioxide tension (PaCO2). This is the most common form of respiratory failure. It can be associated with virtually all acute diseases of the lung. Some examples of type I respiratory failure are cardiogenic or noncardiogenic pulmonary edema, pneumonia, and pulmonary hemorrhage.

Hypercapnic respiratory failure (type II) is characterized by a PaCO2 higher than 50 mm Hg. In many cases, hypercapnic and hypoxemic respiratory failure coexist. Hypoxemia is common in patients with hypercapnic respiratory failure who are breathing room air. Common etiologies include drug overdose, neuromuscular disease, chest wall abnormalities, and severe airway disorders (eg, asthma and chronic obstructive pulmonary disease).

Pulmonary edema is most often a result of acute decompensated heart failure. Fluid transudation is mediated by a rise in pulmonary capillary pressure that results from an increase in pulmonary venous and left atrial pressure. There is filtration of protein-poor liquid across the pulmonary endothelium into the pulmonary interstitium. In the initial stages, the accumulation of liquid in the lung interstitium leads to mild hypoxemia. Tachypnea at this stage is mainly the result of the stimulation of juxtapulmonary capillary (J-type) receptors, which are nonmyelinated nerve endings located near the alveoli. As fluid accumulates in the relatively noncompliant interstitial space, the fluid crosses the alveolar epithelium into the alveoli, leading to alveolar flooding. At this stage, hypoxemia becomes more severe. Tachypnea keeps the PCO2 level low or normal.

Pulmonary embolism (PE) - Impaired gas exchange causes hypoxemia. Arterial blood gas determinations characteristically reveal hypoxemia, *hypocapnia*, and respiratory alkalosis. Unexplained hypoxemia in the setting of a normal chest radiograph should raise the clinical suspicion for PE and prompt further evaluation.

Hypercapnia, respiratory, and/or lactic acidosis are uncommon but can be seen in patients with massive PE associated with obstructive shock and respiratory arrest.

48) A 60-year-old man with pneumonia is unconscious and has a PaO2 of 50 mm Hg. What is the treatment?
   a. Oxygen through nasal cannula
   b. Noninvasive ventilation
   c. Invasive mechanical ventilation
   d. No respiratory support is indicated

   Ans: (c)

Hypoxemic respiratory failure (type I) is characterized by an arterial oxygen tension (PaO2) lower than 60 mm Hg with a normal or low arterial carbon dioxide tension (PaCO2). This can be associated with virtually all acute diseases of the lung. The first objective in the management of respiratory failure is to reverse and/or prevent tissue hypoxia.

Arterial oxygen tension <50 mm Hg on room air indicates the need for mechanical ventilation. In a comatose patient, invasive mechanical ventilation is needed. A cuffed endotracheal tube is necessary, to prevent aspiration of oropharyngeal or gastrointestinal contents in the comatose patient (depressed protective laryngeal reflexes and incomplete glottic inlet closure).

Non-invasive ventilation (NIV) refers to positive pressure ventilation delivered through a non-invasive interface (nasal mask, facemask, or nasal plugs), rather than an invasive interface (endotracheal tube, tracheostomy). Its use has become more common as its benefits are increasingly recognized. Severely impaired consciousness is an absolute contraindication to NIV.

Extracorporeal membrane oxygenation (ECMO) may be more effective than conventional management for patients with severe but potentially reversible respiratory failure.

49) Ventilator induced lung injuries: (Multiple correct answers)
   a. Volutrauma
   b. Barotrauma
   c. Biotrauma
   d. Atelectruma
   e. Atelectasis

Ans: (a, b, c & d)

Ventilator-induced lung injury (VILI)

VILI is an acute lung injury affecting the airways and parenchyma that is caused by or exacerbated by mechanical ventilation. Alveolar overdistension, atelectrauma, and biotrauma are the principal mechanisms of VILI, although the relative contribution of each is unknown. Alveolar injury results in high alveolar permeability, interstitial and alveolar edema, alveolar hemorrhage, hyaline membranes, loss of functional surfactant, and alveolar collapse (ie, ARDS).

Alveolar overdistension (volutrauma)

Volutrauma represents lung injury caused as lung units are overdistended with increased transpulmonary pressure. High tidal volumes (or high lung volumes), rather than high airway pressure per se, cause lung injury.

Large tidal volumes are not always required for alveolar overdistension. When there is consolidation or atelectasis (eg, patient with ARDS), a disproportionate volume from each breath is delivered to the open alveoli. This can cause regional alveolar overdistension and VILI despite delivery of conventional tidal volumes that are based upon body weight.

Atelectrauma

Cyclic alveolar expansion (during inspiration) and collapse (during expiration) creates shear forces that distend and cause injury to adjacent alveoli and airways. Non-atelectatic alveoli are exposed to the injurious impact of neighboring atelectatic alveoli that are opening and collapsing during tidal breathing. This process is referred to as cyclical atelectasis, or atelectrauma.

Barotrauma

Barotrauma refers to alveolar rupture due to elevated transalveolar pressure. All patients on mechanical ventilation are at risk of barotrauma.

Biotrauma (inflammation)

Biotrauma is characterized by ventilator-induced release of inflammatory mediators from cells within the injured lung. Both alveolar overdistension and atelectrauma result in an increase in inflammatory mediators.

50) False about transfusion associated fluid overload
   a. Can occur with transfusion of any blood component
   b. Pre-existing cardiac dysfunction is a risk factor
   c. Hypoxia is common
   d. BNP is low

   Ans: (d)

Transfusion-associated circulatory overload (TACO) is a form of circulatory volume overload that can occur with transfusion of any blood component (eg, RBCs, platelets, FFP or other plasma product, cryoprecipitate). Risk factors include pre-existing cardiac and renal dysfunction, extremes of age, low body weight, greater number of units transfused, and faster rate of infusion.

The possibility of TACO should be considered in any patient who has respiratory distress (dyspnea, orthopnea) or hypertension during or within six hours of completing a transfusion, especially in individuals with underlying heart disease.

Findings consistent with TACO include hypoxia, jugular venous distention, pulmonary rales, an S3 gallop, pulmonary edema on chest radiography, and elevated BNP or NT-BNP.

Differentiation between TACO and TRALI is aided with the use of brain natriuretic peptide (BNP). In transfusion-related circulatory overload, the BNP will be elevated, whereas in patients with TRALI, there will be no elevation of BNP.

51) A patient in the ICU was given a blood transfusion. 3 hours later, the patient developed dyspnea. PaO2/FiO2 is ≤300 mg Hg. Pretransfusion (a) and posttransfusion (b) chest X-rays are shown below. What is the diagnosis?

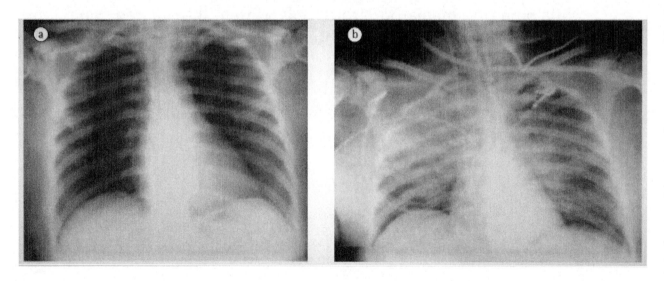

    a. Tension pneumothorax
    b. Transfusion associated lung injury
    c. Mismatch blood transfusion
    d. Circulatory overload

Ans: (b). The chest x-ray shows bilateral patchy infiltrates.

Transfusion-related acute lung injury (TRALI) is the most commonly encountered serious complication of transfusion therapy and is the leading cause of transfusion-related death. TRALI is clinically defined as noncardiogenic pulmonary edema after a blood product transfusion without other explanation. Plasma-containing products are most frequently implicated (50 to 63 percent of TRALI fatalities). TRALI usually results from the transfusion of donor plasma that contains high-titer anti-HLA class II antibodies that bind recipient leukocytes. The leukocytes aggregate in the pulmonary vasculature and release mediators that increase capillary permeability.

Symptoms develop within 6 hours of transfusion. Dyspnea is the primary presenting symptom. Other symptoms are frothy sputum, hypotension, fever, and tachycardia. Diffuse bilateral pulmonary infiltrates on chest radiography is characteristic.

Diagnosis

TRALI is a clinical diagnosis. See table below.

Diagnostic criteria for TRALI

TRALI
▪ Acute onset (during or within six hours of transfusion)
▪ Hypoxemia*
▪ Bilateral infiltrates on frontal chest radiograph
▪ No evidence of circulatory overload/left atrial hypertension
▪ No pre-existing ALI/ARDS before transfusion

* Hypoxemia is defined as PaO2/FiO2 ≤300 or SpO2 <90 percent on room air or other clinical evidence of hypoxemia.

For a diagnosis of TRALI to be made, all of these features must be present. In addition, there should be no preexisting ALI/ARDS risk factors at the time of transfusion. Risk factors include aspiration, toxic inhalation, pneumonia, toxic contusion, near drowning, shock states, severe sepsis, multiple trauma, burn injury, acute pancreatitis, cardiopulmonary bypass, or drug overdose.

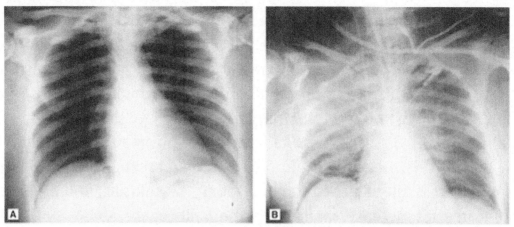

Development of TRALI following blood transfusion. A) Before transfusion. B) After transfusion showing rapid emergence of bilateral pulmonary infiltrates.

Treatment

When a transfusion reaction such as TRALI is suspected, the transfusion should be stopped immediately. Oxygen supplementation for the correction of hypoxemia is the cornerstone of treatment. The majority of patients who develop TRALI will require ICU admission and ventilator support for 3 to 10 days.

No evidence supports the routine use of corticosteroids.

52) False about transfusion related acute lung injury (TRALI)
    a. Survivors can safely receive additional blood products in the future
    b. Complete recovery may take up to 3 days
    c. Supportive care is the mainstay of treatment
    d. Steroids have doubtful role in management

    Ans: (b)

TRALI is clinically defined as noncardiogenic pulmonary edema after a blood product transfusion without other explanation. Plasma-containing products are most frequently implicated (50 to 63 percent of TRALI fatalities). TRALI usually results from the transfusion of donor plasma that contains high-titer anti-HLA class II antibodies that bind recipient leukocytes. The leukocytes aggregate in the pulmonary vasculature and release mediators that increase capillary permeability.

Symptoms develop within 6 hours of transfusion. Dyspnea is the primary presenting symptom. Other symptoms are frothy sputum, hypotension, fever, and tachycardia. Diffuse bilateral pulmonary infiltrates on chest radiography is characteristic.

Diagnosis
TRALI is a clinical diagnosis. See table below.

Diagnostic criteria for TRALI

TRALI

- Acute onset (during or within six hours of transfusion)
- Hypoxemia*
- Bilateral infiltrates on frontal chest radiograph
- No evidence of circulatory overload/left atrial hypertension
- No pre-existing ALI/ARDS before transfusion

For a diagnosis of TRALI to be made, all of these features must be present. In addition, there should be no preexisting ALI/ARDS risk factors at the time of transfusion. Risk factors include aspiration, toxic inhalation, pneumonia, toxic contusion, near drowning, shock states, severe sepsis, multiple trauma, burn injury, acute pancreatitis, cardiopulmonary bypass, or drug overdose. If ALI/ARDS risk factors are present, the diagnostic terminology "possible TRALI" is appropriate.
* Hypoxemia is defined as PaO2/FiO2 ≤300 or SpO2 <90 percent on room air or other clinical evidence of hypoxemia.

Treatment

When a transfusion reaction such as TRALI is suspected, the transfusion should be stopped immediately. Oxygen supplementation for the correction of hypoxemia is the cornerstone of treatment. The majority of patients who develop TRALI will require ICU admission and ventilator support for 3 to 10 days.

No evidence supports the routine use of corticosteroids.

Most survivors will recover to their baseline pulmonary function, and they can safely receive additional blood products in the future.

53) You are present at bedside of patient who is being intubated and ventilated. On examination patient's EtCO2 value shows zero. Which of the following can be the reason?   Multiple Correct Answers
   a. Endotracheal tube in esophagus
   b. Endotracheal tube extubation
   c. Pulmonary embolism
   d. Ventilator circuit break
   e. Ventilator disconnected

Ans: (a, b, d & e)

Capnography and EtCO2

The term capnography refers to the noninvasive measurement of the partial pressure of carbon dioxide in exhaled breath. EtCO2 is end-tidal CO_2. Capnography provides instantaneous information about ventilation (how effectively CO2 is being eliminated by the pulmonary system), perfusion (how effectively CO2 is being transported through the vascular system), and metabolism (how effectively CO2 is being produced by cellular metabolism).

Capnography is the most reliable indicator that an endotracheal tube is placed in the trachea after intubation. Misplacement of the tracheal tube in the esophagus or right main bronchus is a major cause of avoidable anesthetic morbidity and mortality. Immediate confirmation of correct tracheal tube placement is an essential part of tracheal intubation. Identification of CO_2 in the expired gas is the standard for verification of proper tracheal tube placement. Persistent detection of CO_2 by a capnograph is the best confirmation of tracheal placement.

Accidental bronchial intubation can occur during intubation or subsequently. This complication can occur especially if head flexion is increased after initial tracheal tube fixation, the diaphragm is elevated by increased intra-abdominal pressure, or a head-down position is used.

The earliest manifestation of bronchial intubation is an increase in peak inspiratory pressure. The most important sign is hypoxemia, usually combined with increased airway pressure. Bronchial intubation is also suggested by asymmetric chest expansion. Absence of breath sounds over one lung strongly suggests bronchial intubation. Inability to palpate the tracheal tube cuff in the sternal notch during cuff inflation and decreased breathing-bag compliance (high peak inspiratory pressures) are other clues.

Preventing unintentional esophageal intubation depends on direct visualization of the tip of the tracheal tube passing through the vocal cords, careful auscultation for the presence of bilateral breath sounds and the absence of gastric gurgling, analysis of exhaled gas for the presence of CO_2 (the most reliable method), chest radiography, or use of fiberoptic bronchoscopy.

Infections

54) Virus causing acute severe respiratory distress
    a. RSV
    b. Coronavirus
    c. H1N1
    d. Measles

Ans: (b)

Severe acute respiratory syndrome (SARS)

A novel coronavirus is the cause of SARS. Coronaviruses are usually agents of the common cold and generally do not cause severe respiratory disease. It has been classified as a lineage B beta-coronavirus (with several bat coronaviruses).

SARS is an unusual respiratory viral disease since the prodrome is often somewhat prolonged, lasting for three to seven days, and is characterized by fever, malaise, headache, and myalgias. Unlike virtually all other respiratory viral prodromes, most patients have no upper respiratory symptoms during this stage. At the end of this prodrome, the respiratory phase typically begins with a non-productive cough. Dyspnea may follow and may progress to respiratory failure, with progressive pulmonary infiltrates on chest radiograph, necessitating mechanical ventilation.

H1N1 virus

H1N1 virus is a genetic reassortment of swine, human, and avian strains of influenza. Typical clinical manifestations of H1N1 influenza A infection include fever, headache, cough, sore throat, myalgias, chills, and fatigue; vomiting and diarrhea are also common, both of which are unusual features of seasonal influenza. Disease severity ranges from mild influenza-like illness to multiorgan failure with severe hypoxemia. Individuals with certain medical conditions, those at the extremes of age, and pregnant women were at increased risk of influenza complications, including respiratory failure.

55) True regarding metapneumovirus is:
   a. Segmented negative sense single stranded RNA virus
   b. Spreads through sexual contact and blood transfusion
   c. Human metapneumovirus contains NS1 and NS2 antigens
   d. Antiviral therapy with oseltamivir is recommended

   Ans: (a)

Human metapneumovirus (hMPV) is a single negative-stranded RNA-enveloped virus classified in the Pneumovirinae subfamily of the Paramyxoviridae family. Influenza viruses, RSV, and hMPV are the most common causes of serious lower respiratory tract disease in otherwise healthy subjects.

Transmission of HMPV is by direct or close contact with contaminated secretions, not small particle aerosols. The incubation period is thought to be five to nine days in most cases, with a typical duration of illness of approximately one week.

HMPV is usually associated with mild, self-limited infections in children and adults. Among patients who require hospitalization, clinical manifestations can range from bronchiolitis or asthma exacerbation to severe pneumonia and acute respiratory distress syndrome.
Reverse-transcriptase polymerase chain reaction (PCR) on nasopharyngeal specimens is the most sensitive method for diagnosis of hMPV infection. Treatment is supportive. Antiviral therapy is not recommended.

Dengue viruses contain NS1 and NS2 antigens.

56) Not recommended for worsening respiratory distress in a child with acute croup
   a. Sedation
   b. Intravenous antibiotics
   c. Nebulized racemic epinephrine
   d. Intramuscular dexamethasone

Ans: (a)

Croup (laryngotracheitis) is a respiratory illness characterized by inspiratory stridor, barking cough, and hoarseness. It typically occurs in children six months to three years of age and is chiefly caused by parainfluenza virus. Most children with croup have a mild, self-limited illness and can be successfully managed as outpatients.

Treatment

Mild croup, signified by a barking cough and no stridor at rest, requires supportive therapy with oral hydration and minimal handling. Patients with stridor at rest require active intervention. Oxygen should be administered to patients with oxygen desaturation. Current standard treatment is the use of nebulized epinephrine and corticosteroids (see table below).

Nebulized epinephrine is the mainstay of treatment for moderate to severe croup patients with marked retractions and stridor at rest. Mild croup generally does not require epinephrine. Epinephrine works by rapidly decreasing airway edema through vasoconstrictive alpha effects.

Children with mild, moderate, and severe croup all benefit from corticosteroids, which reduce both the severity and duration of croup episodes. Corticosteroids improve symptoms by anti-inflammatory effects in the upper airway.

Dexamethasone, 0.6 mg/kg intramuscularly as one dose, improves symptoms, reduces the duration of hospitalizations and frequency of intubations, and permits earlier discharge from the emergency department. Oral dexamethasone (0.15 mg/kg) is equally effective.

Inhaled budesonide (2–4 mg) also improves symptoms and decreases hospital stay. Onset of action occurs within 2 hours, and this agent may be as effective as dexamethasone.

Patients with impending respiratory failure require an artificial airway. Intubation is reserved for cases of severe croup not responding to medical treatment. When intubation is necessary, use endotracheal tubes smaller than recommended for patient size and age to avoid traumatizing the inflamed mucosa.

Beta-agonists such as salbutamol (albuterol) should not be used for croup or when signs of upper airway obstruction from edema are present (i.e., stridor). Vascular beta-receptors cause vasodilation that may worsen edema and exacerbate upper airway obstruction.

Croup Pharmacotherapy

Medication	Dose	Notes
Dexamethasone	0.15–0.6 milligrams/kg PO/IM (10 milligrams maximum)	Give for mild, moderate, or severe croup. May crush pills and mix in juice or applesauce. May give IV solution PO without dilution.
Budesonide	2 milligrams nebulized	Consider if PO steroids vomited.
L-epinephrine (1:1000)	0.5 mL/kg nebulized (5 mL maximum)	Use for moderate or severe croup; may need repeat dose if severe.
Racemic epinephrine (2.25%)	0.05 mL/kg/dose nebulized (maximum 0.5 mL)	Use for moderate or severe croup; may need repeat dose if severe.

57) Most important sign of severe pneumonia in a child
   a. Fast breathing

b. Nasal flaring
c. Chest indrawing
d. Grunting

Ans: (a)

Newborns with pneumonia rarely cough; they more commonly present with poor feeding and irritability, as well as tachypnea, retractions, grunting, and hypoxemia. Grunting in a new-born suggests a lower respiratory tract disease; it is due to vocal cord approximation as they try to provide increased positive end-expiratory pressure (PEEP) and keep their lower airways open.

After the first month of life, cough is the most common presenting symptom of pneumonia. Tachypnea, retractions, and hypoxemia are common. Grunting may be less common in older infants.

Toddlers and pre-schoolers most often present with fever, cough (productive or non-productive), tachypnea, and congestion.

Tachypnea is the most sensitive finding in patients with diagnosed pneumonia. Signs such as grunting, flaring, severe tachypnea, and retractions should prompt the clinician to provide immediate respiratory support. Retractions result from the effort to increase intrathoracic pressure to compensate for decreased compliance.

Severity of community-acquired pneumonia in infants and children

Mild pneumonia	Severe pneumonia
Temperature <38.5°C (101.3°F)	Temperature ≥38.5°C (101.3°F)
Mild or absent respiratory distress: • Increased RR, but less than the	Moderate to severe respiratory distress:

age-specific RR that defines moderate to severe respiratory distress - Mild or absent retractions - No grunting - No nasal flaring - No apnea - Mild shortness of breath	- RR >70 breaths/minute for infants; RR >50 breaths/minute for older children - Moderate/severe suprasternal, intercostal, or subcostal retractions (<12 months) - Severe difficulty breathing (≥12 months) - Grunting - Nasal flaring - Apnea - Significant shortness of breath
Normal color	Cyanosis
Normal mental status	Altered mental status
Normoxemia (oxygen saturation ≥92 percent in room air)	Hypoxemia (sustained oxygen saturation <90 percent in room air at sea level)
Normal feeding (infants); no vomiting	Not feeding (infants) or signs of dehydration (older children)
Normal heart rate	Tachycardia
Capillary refill <2 seconds	Capillary refill ≥2 seconds

Care in the intensive care unit may be warranted for children with two or more of the following:
- Respiratory rate >70 breaths/minute for infants <12 months of age and >50 breaths/minute for older children
- Apnea
- Increased work of breathing (retractions, dyspnea, nasal flaring, grunting)
- Partial pressure of oxygen in arterial blood (PaO2)/FiO2 ratio <250
- Multilobar infiltrates

- Altered mental status
- Hypotension
- Pleural effusion
- Comorbid condition (eg, sickle cell disease, immune deficiency, immunosuppression)

58) Gross specimen of lung from a patient is shown below. What is the diagnosis?

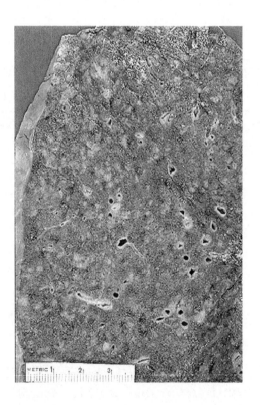

    a. Pneumoconiosis
    b. Miliary tuberculosis
    c. Bronchiectasis
    d. Pneumonia

Ans: (b)

Miliary tuberculosis results from the hematogenous dissemination of Mycobacterium tuberculosis; it affects multiple organs and systems. Classic miliary TB is defined as millet-like (mean, 2 mm; range, 1-5 mm) seeding of TB bacilli in the lung, as evidenced on chest radiography.

"Miliary" pattern of granulomas - there are a number of small granulomas, about 2 to 4 mm in size, scattered throughout the lung parenchyma. The miliary pattern gets its name from the resemblance of the granulomas to millet seeds.

Granuloma - Focal collection of inflammatory cells at sites of tissue infection and includes activated macrophages (epithelioid cells), Langhans' giant cells, and lymphocytes.

Caseation necrosis - Regions in granulomas with eosinophilic, granular, and friable (cheese-like) cellular debris with necrosis

Granulomatous inflammation - A distinctive pattern of chronic inflammatory reaction characterized by focal accumulation of activated macrophages (epithelioid histiocytes)

59) False regarding ventilator associated pneumonia:
   a. Progressive lung infiltrate on imaging
   b. Clinical evidence of infection
   c. Mechanical ventilation for at least 3 days
   d. BAL culture

   Ans: (c)

Ventilator-associated pneumonia (VAP) is pneumonia that develops 48 hours or longer after mechanical ventilation is given by means of an endotracheal tube or tracheostomy. Intubation compromises the integrity of the oropharynx and trachea and allows oral and gastric secretions to enter the lower airways.

VAP is a clinical diagnosis based upon:
- Identification a new or progressive lung infiltrate on imaging
- Clinical evidence of infection
  - Fever
  - Purulent sputum
  - Leukocytosis
  - Decline in oxygenation
- Positive pathogen identified on microbiologic respiratory sample. VAP cannot be confirmed or excluded until the culture results are complete, which generally takes two to three days.

60) Causative organism for ventilator associated pneumonia
   a. Clostridium
   b. P aeruginosa
   c. Staphylococcus epidermidis
   d. Legionella

   Ans: (b)

Ventilator-associated pneumonia (VAP) is a type of hospital-acquired pneumonia (HAP) that develops after more than 48 hours of mechanical ventilation (endotracheal intubation). The primary route of infection of the lungs is through microaspiration of organisms that have colonized the oropharyngeal tract (or to a lesser extent the gastrointestinal tract).

Organisms associated with VAP include the following:
- P aeruginosa
- S Aureus
- S maltophilia
- Acinetobacter species
- Enterobacteriaceae are less commonly seen in VAP than in hospital-acquired pneumonia

Anaerobic organisms are not important pathogens in nosocomial pneumonia.

Typically, bacteria causing early-onset VAP include Streptococcus pneumoniae streptococcus species), Hemophilus influenzae, methicillin-sensitive Staphylococcus aureus (MSSA), antibiotic-sensitive enteric Gram-negative bacilli, Escherichia coli, Klebsiella pneumonia, Enterobacter species, Proteus species and Serratia marcescens. Culprits of late VAP are typically MDR bacteria, such as methicillin-resistant S. aureus (MRSA), Acinetobacter, Pseudomonas aeruginosa, and extended-spectrum beta-lactamase producing bacteria (ESBL). The exact prevalence of MDR organisms is variable between institutions and also within institutions.

61) Treatment of ventilator associated pneumonia (VAP) caused by MDR Acinetobacter baumannii is:
   a. Quinupristin/dalfopristin
   b. Colistin
   c. Lavendamycin
   d. Tedizolid

   Ans: (b)

Acinetobacter baumannii is one of the ESKAPE organisms; these are a group of predominantly health care-associated organisms that have the potential for substantial antimicrobial resistance. Other ESKAPE organisms are Enterococcus faecium, Staphylococcus aureus, Klebsiella pneumoniae, Pseudomonas aeruginosa, and Enterobacter species.

Acinetobacter is a gram-negative coccobacillus that has the ability to accumulate diverse mechanisms of resistance, leading to the emergence of strains that are resistant to all commercially available antibiotics. A baumannii is inherently resistant to multiple antibiotics.

Most Acinetobacter isolates are recovered from hospitalized patients. Multiple factors tend to increase the risk for acquiring an Acinetobacter infection, including prior antibiotic exposure, intensive care unit admission, use of a central venous catheter, and mechanical ventilation or hemodialysis use. Acinetobacter pneumonias occur in outbreaks and are usually associated with colonized respiratory-support equipment or fluids.

When infections are caused by antibiotic-susceptible Acinetobacter isolates, there may be several therapeutic options, including a broad-spectrum cephalosporin (ceftazidime or cefepime), a combination beta-lactam/beta-lactamase inhibitor (ie, one that includes sulbactam), or a carbapenem (eg, imipenem, meropenem, or doripenem). In the setting of resistance to the above agents, therapeutic options are polymyxins and possibly tigecycline.

For patients with infections due to extensively drug-resistant Acinetobacter, therapeutic options are generally limited to polymyxins (colistin and polymyxin B), minocycline, and tigecycline.

Quinupristin/dalfopristin is a combination of two antibiotics used to treat infections by staphylococci and by vancomycin-resistant Enterococcus faecium. While each of the two is only a bacteriostatic agent, the combination shows bactericidal activity.

Tedizolid is used for the treatment of acute bacterial skin infections and skin structure infections caused by certain susceptible bacteria, including staphylococcus aureus (including methicillin-resistant strains and methicillin-susceptible strains), various streptococcus species and Enterococcus faecalis. Tedizolid is 4-to-16-fold more potent against staphylococci compared to linezolid.

Lavendamycin has no clinical uses.

62) Most common cause of lung infection in an adult smoker with consolidation
   a. Streptococcus pneumoniae
   b. Klebsiella
   c. Staphylococcus
   d. Burkholderia

Ans: (a)

In patients with COPD, chronic infection or colonization of the lower airways is common from S pneumoniae, H influenzae, and M catarrhalis.

63) Least common cause of lung cavitation
   a. Lung cancer
   b. Pulmonary embolism
   c. Klebsiella pneumoniae
   d. Wegener's granulomatosis

Ans: (b)

Cavitary Pulmonary Disease

A pulmonary cavity is a lucency within a zone of pulmonary consolidation, a mass, or a nodule that may or may not contain a fluid level and that is surrounded by a wall, usually of varied thickness.

A cavity is the result of any of a number of pathological processes including suppurative necrosis (e.g., pyogenic lung abscess), caseous

81

necrosis (e.g., tuberculosis), ischemic necrosis (e.g., pulmonary infarction), cystic dilatation of lung structures (e.g., ball valve obstruction and Pneumocystis pneumonia), or displacement of lung tissue by cystic structures (e.g., Echinococcus). In addition, malignant processes may cavitate.

Infections associated with lung cavities

Klebsiella pneumoniae is a common cause of severe, necrotizing pneumonia. K. pneumoniae pneumonia is frequently complicated by lung abscess, which generally appears as one or more cavities.

Staphylococcus aureus is another common cause of cavitary pneumonia. Septic pulmonary emboli associated with intravenous drug use are caused predominantly by S. aureus.

Mycobacterium tuberculosis is a quite common cause of lung cavity. See the x-ray below.

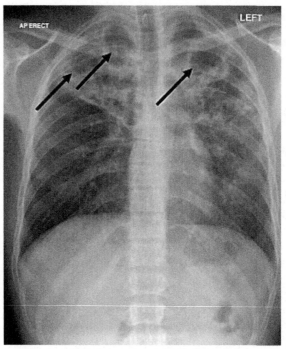

Extensive cavitary lung disease due to Mycobacterium tuberculosis. Note the typical upper lobe predominance and extensive fibronodular infiltrates.

Primary lung cancer is a common malignant etiology of a lung cavity. Cavitation is more frequently found among cases of squamous cell carcinomas than other histological types. Other primary tumors in the lung, such as lymphoma and Kaposi's sarcoma, may also present with cavitary lesions, particularly among persons infected with human immunodeficiency virus. See the x-ray below.

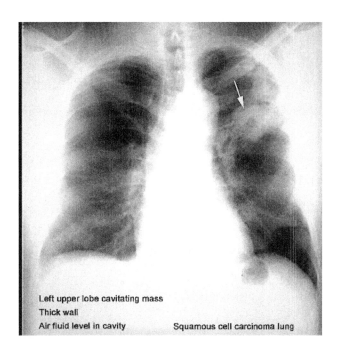

Left upper lobe cavitating mass
Thick wall
Air fluid level in cavity   Squamous cell carcinoma lung

Metastatic disease from other primary sites may also cavitate, but this occurs less frequently than in primary lung cancers.

Wegener's granulomatosis is an uncommon disorder in which cavitary lung disease is frequently encountered. Pulmonary cavities have been observed by computed tomography in 35 to 50% of patients with Wegener's granulomatosis involving the lung. Wegener's granulomatosis is a systemic vasculitis that almost always involves the upper or lower respiratory tract.

Pulmonary embolism is usually associated with nonspecific radiographic changes or even a normal chest radiograph. Pulmonary infarction and necrosis may infrequently result in a cavitary lesion.

64) Causes of chronic empyema: (Multiple correct answers)

a. Drainage of pleural effusion
b. Inadequate antibiotic treatment for acute empyema
c. Inadequate needle aspiration of acute empyema
d. Vigorous chest physiotherapy
e. Ruptured subphrenic abscess

Ans: (a, b, c & e)

Empyema develops when there is bacterial infection of the pleural liquid, resulting in either pus or the presence of bacterial organisms on Gram stain. Empyema most commonly occurs in the setting of underlying suppurative lung disease (ie, pneumonia, lung abscess, or bronchiectasis).

Other causes of thoracic empyema are surgery (20%), trauma (10%), esophageal rupture, other chest wall or mediastinal infections, bronchopleural fistula, extension of a subphrenic or hepatic abscess, instrumentation of the pleural space (thoracentesis, chest tube placement, etc), and, rarely, hematogenous seeding from a distant site of infection.

Mycobacterium tuberculosis, Nocardia asteroids, and fungi are other causes.

65) An adult male has fever and right sided chest pain. Chest x-ray shows a moderate pleural effusion on the right side. A diagnostic thoracentesis reveals straw colored exudates with 40 mg% of sugar and lymphocytic pleocytosis. ADA levels are borderline. Which investigation would be most likely to confirm a diagnosis of tuberculosis?
a. Needle biopsy of the pleura
b. Pleural fluid Xpert MTB/RIF assay
c. Pleural fluid AFB smear
d. Pleural fluid AFB culture

Ans: (a)

The most common cause of an exudative pleural effusion in India is tuberculosis. Tuberculous pleural effusion is the second most common form of extrapulmonary tuberculosis (after lymphatic involvement).

Development of tuberculous pleural effusion occurs most commonly as a result of delayed hypersensitivity reaction to mycobacteria or mycobacterial antigens in the pleural space. Less commonly, tuberculous pleural effusion develops when a subpleural focus of disease ruptures into the pleural space

The diagnosis of tuberculous pleuritis remains a challenge because of the small numbers of bacilli in the pleural fluid. Patients with tuberculous pleuritis present with fever, weight loss, dyspnea, and/or pleuritic chest pain.

Pleural fluid lymphocytosis
Pleural fluid lymphocytosis, with lymphocyte values greater than 85% of the total nucleated cells, suggests TB, lymphoma, sarcoidosis, chronic rheumatoid pleurisy, yellow nail syndrome, and chylothorax. Pleural lymphocyte values of 50-70% of the nucleated cells suggests malignancy.

A low pleural glucose concentration (30-50 mg/dL) suggests malignant effusion, tuberculous pleuritis, esophageal rupture, or lupus pleuritis. A very low pleural glucose concentration (ie, < 30 mg/dL) further restricts diagnostic possibilities, to rheumatoid pleurisy or empyema.

The diagnosis is established by demonstrating high levels of TB markers in the pleural fluid (adenosine deaminase >40 IU/L or interferon γ >140 pg/mL). Alternatively, the diagnosis can be established by culture of the pleural fluid, needle biopsy of the pleura, or thoracoscopy.

Pleural fluid staining for AFB and culture has low sensitivity and culture takes more than a week even when using automated systems. Because most tuberculous pleural effusions result from a hypersensitivity reaction to the Mycobacterium rather than from microbial invasion of the pleura, acid-fast bacillus stains of pleural fluid are rarely diagnostic (< 10% of cases). Pleural fluid cultures grow M tuberculosis in less than 65% of cases.

Adenosine deaminase (ADA) is a protein that is produced by cells throughout the body and is associated with the activation of lymphocytes. Conditions that trigger the immune system, such as an infection by Mycobacterium tuberculosis, may cause increased amounts of ADA to be produced in the areas where the bacteria are present.

Adenosine deaminase activity (ADA) is a commonly used marker for the diagnosis of tuberculous pleural effusion. The ADA assay is inexpensive, rapid, and simple to perform and is of great value for the immediate diagnosis of tuberculous pleuritis while waiting for culture result.

Adenosine deaminase activity of greater than 43 U/mL in pleural fluid supports the diagnosis of tuberculous pleuritis. However, the test has a sensitivity of only 78%. Therefore, pleural ADA values of less than 43-50 U/mL do not exclude the diagnosis of TB pleuritis.

Currently, the best tool for diagnosing tuberculous pleural effusion is a thoracoscopic pleural biopsy, an invasive procedure, with sensitivity ranging from 93 to 100%.

Pleural biopsy is warranted if the pleural fluid ADA level is <40 units/L and/or pleural fluid evaluation is otherwise not diagnostic. Pleural biopsy should be sent for AFB smear and culture as well as histopathologic evaluation. Histopathology may demonstrate granulomas and/or acid-fast bacilli. The presence of caseating (necrotizing) granulomas on histologic examination is virtually diagnostic of tuberculous pleural effusion. The combination of histology and culture of pleural tissue obtained by pleural biopsy increases the diagnostic yield for TB to 90%. However, the invasiveness of the procedure, inability to get representative pleural tissue and the risk of complications are limitations in obtaining pleural biopsies.

CT of the thorax

CT imaging of the thorax with pleural phase contrast enhancement should be performed in virtually all patients with an undiagnosed pleural effusion. Irregular or thickened pleura with contrast enhancement suggests pleural inflammation or malignancy and identifies optimal sites for CT-guided needle aspiration or cutting needle biopsy.

Nucleic Acid Amplification Tests (NAATs)

NAATs are available for the rapid and direct detection of M tuberculosis in clinical specimens. The GeneXpert MTB/RIF test is a real-time multiplex PCR method that both identify the DNA in mycobacteria complex and also rifampicin resistance (detects genes that encode rifampin resistance).

Xpert MTB/RIF assay

The Xpert MTB/RIF assay can make a rapid diagnosis of TB disease and drug resistance. The test simultaneously detects Mycobacterium tuberculosis complex and resistance to rifampin in less than 2 hours. A negative result is not sufficient to exclude the presence of active TB or drug resistance.

The Xpert MTB/RIF assay can quickly identify possible multidrug-resistant TB (MDR TB). MDR TB is TB that is resistant to both INH and RIF. RIF resistance is a predictor of MDR TB because resistance to RIF, in most instances co-exists with resistance to INH. Rapid diagnosis of RIF resistance potentially allows TB patients to start on effective treatment much sooner than waiting for results from other types of drug susceptibility testing.

Xpert MTB/RIF has poor sensitivity for the diagnosis of tuberculous pleural effusion. The sensitivity and specificity of the Xpert assay in pleural fluid are 50% and 99%, respectively. Given its high specificity, it can potentially obviate the need for an invasive procedure in at least one-fourth of patients with tuberculous pleural effusion.

66) A 26-year-old presents with pleural effusion due to suspected tuberculosis. You will analyze the pleural fluid for all of the parameters except-
   a. Gene Xpert
   b. LDH
   c. Albumin
   d. ADA (adenosine deaminase)

Ans: (c)

The diagnosis of tuberculous pleuritis remains a challenge because of the small numbers of bacilli in the pleural fluid. The diagnosis is established by demonstrating high levels of TB markers in the pleural fluid (adenosine deaminase >40 IU/L or interferon γ >140 pg/mL). Alternatively, the diagnosis can be established by culture of the pleural fluid, needle biopsy of the pleura, or thoracoscopy.

Pleural fluid staining for AFB and culture has low sensitivity and culture takes more than a week even when using automated systems. Pleural biopsy culture and typical histology of necrotizing granuloma is more sensitive than pleural fluid culture. However, the invasiveness of the procedure, inability to get representative pleural tissue and the risk of complications are limitations in obtaining pleural biopsies.

Nucleic Acid Amplification Tests (NAATs) are available for the rapid and direct detection of M tuberculosis in clinical specimens. The GeneXpert MTB/RIF test is a real-time multiplex PCR method that both identify the DNA in mycobacteria complex and also rifampicin resistance (detects genes that encode rifampin resistance).

Adenosine Deaminase Activity (ADA) is a commonly used marker for the diagnosis of tuberculous pleural effusion. The ADA assay is inexpensive, rapid, and simple to perform and is of great value for the immediate diagnosis of tuberculous pleuritis while waiting for culture result.

Adenosine deaminase is a protein that is produced by cells throughout the body and is associated with the activation of lymphocytes. Conditions that trigger the immune system, such as an infection by Mycobacterium tuberculosis, may cause increased amounts of ADA to be produced in the areas where the bacteria are present.

The test most useful to differentiate transudate from exudate is LDH. Pleural liquid LDH arises from filtration from serum and therefore, they are indicators of vascular permeability. LDH is an intracellular enzyme and therefore, may also indicate the degree of cell turnover and/or the degree of inflammation within the pleural space. The level of LDH in the pleural fluid reflects the degree of inflammation in the pleural space. If the pleural fluid LDH concentration increases with serial thoracentesis, it means that the degree of inflammation in the pleural space is worsening. Alternatively, if the pleural fluid LDH level decrease with serial thoracentesis, the pleural disease is resolving, and observation of the patient is indicated.

Pleural fluid LDH levels greater than 1000 IU/L suggest empyema, malignant effusion, rheumatoid effusion, or pleural paragonimiasis. Pleural fluid LDH levels are also increased in effusions from Pneumocystis jiroveci pneumonia.

Pleural fluid albumin is not typically measured. A gradient of serum albumin to pleural fluid albumin of less than 1.2 g/dL identifies an exudate.

67) Clinical finding in post-tubercular bronchiectasis
   a. Crackles are mixed (fine as well as course)
   b. Crackles are bibasilar
   c. Crackles are late inspiratory
   d. Tubular type of bronchial breathing is common

   Ans: (a)

Bronchiectasis is abnormal and irreversibly dilated thick-walled bronchi. Bronchiectasis is the end stage of a variety of pathologic processes that cause destruction of the bronchial wall and its surrounding supporting tissues. Bronchiectasis is considered to be idiopathic in up to half of the affected individuals.

More pronounced involvement of the upper lung fields is most common in TB and cystic fibrosis. It is also observed in post-radiation fibrosis, corresponding to the lung region encompassed by the radiation port. Bronchiectasis resulting from infection by nontuberculous mycobacteria, most commonly the Mycobacterium avium-intracellulare complex, often preferentially affects the mid-lung fields.

Bronchiectasis with predominant involvement of the lower lung fields is usually due to chronic recurrent aspiration (e.g., due to esophageal motility disorders like those in scleroderma), end-stage fibrotic lung disease (e.g., traction bronchiectasis from idiopathic pulmonary fibrosis), or recurrent immunodeficiency-associated infections (e.g., hypogammaglobulinemia).

Predominant involvement of the central airways is associated with allergic bronchopulmonary aspergillosis.

The most common clinical presentation is a persistent productive cough with production of copious mucopurulent expectoration. Chest auscultation usually reveals findings of early and mid-inspiratory crackles as well as diffuse rhonchi and prolonged expiration. Bronchial breath sounds may be heard in severe cases or patients with a complicating pneumonia. Digital clubbing and hypertrophic pulmonary osteoarthropathy, although common in the pre-antibiotic era, are rarely seen now.

Coarse crackles are the most common finding in in post-tubercular bronchiectasis. They are heard in early inspiration over the upper lobes.

The diagnosis is based on presentation with a persistent chronic cough and sputum production accompanied by consistent radiographic features. CT is the imaging modality of choice for confirming the diagnosis. Evaluation of focal bronchiectasis almost always requires bronchoscopy to exclude airway obstruction by an underlying mass or foreign body.

68) False about rifabutin as compared to rifampicin
   a. It has higher bioavailability and stronger activity against all mycobacterium
   b. It has a longer half-life
   c. It has lesser drug interactions
   d. It is preferred in patients with HIV

   Ans: (a)

Rifabutin has significant activity against M tuberculosis, MAC, and Mycobacterium fortuitum. Its activity is similar to that of rifampin, and cross-resistance with rifampin is virtually complete.

Rifabutin has reduced potential for drug interactions (relative to rifampin). Therefore, it is most commonly used for treatment of select mycobacterial infections in patients receiving concomitant medications exhibiting significant interactions with rifampin (such as select antiretroviral therapies). Rifampicin induce CYP450 and may decrease substantially blood levels of the antiretroviral drugs. Rifabutin is recommended in place of rifampin for the treatment of HIV-co-infected individuals who are taking protease inhibitors or non-nucleoside reverse transcriptase inhibitors, particularly nevirapine.

Rifabutin's slow clearance results in a serum half-life of 32-67h—much longer than the 2- to 5-h half-life of rifampin.

69) A 40-year-old female presents with fever, cough and hemoptysis of 2 weeks duration. X-rays showed left upper lobe consolidation. Antibiotics were given and fever improved, but

cough and hemoptysis persisted. Bronchoscopy shows a mass filling the left bronchus. What is the likely diagnosis?

    a. Sarcoidosis
    b. Carcinoid
    c. Pulmonary tuberculosis
    d. Hamartoma

Ans: (b)

Carcinoid tumors of the lung

Between 1% and 6% of all lung tumors are carcinoid tumors. Bronchopulmonary carcinoid tumors represent about 10% of all carcinoid tumors. They arise from stem cells of the bronchial epithelium known as Kulchitsky cells. The gastrointestinal tract is the most common area in which carcinoid tumors most commonly arise.

The average age of people at occurrence of typical carcinoid tumors is 40-50 years. Carcinoid tumors occur in equal numbers of males and females.

Carcinoids developing within large airway structures grow slowly and can become quite large. Because of their location and size, these central carcinoids can cause bronchial obstruction. All of the sequelae resulting from bronchial obstruction can follow, including persistent atelectasis, recurrent pneumonia, pulmonary abscess, and bronchiectasis.

Carcinoids characteristically are vascular tumors and can bleed secondary to bronchial irritation.

In symptomatic patients, the most common clinical findings are those associated with bronchial obstruction, such as persistent cough, hemoptysis, and recurrent or obstructive pneumonitis. Wheezing, chest pain, and dyspnea also may be noted.

All pulmonary carcinoid tumors should be treated as malignancies. Total resection should be the primary goal of any form of surgical therapy. Lymph node dissection should accompany resection.

Sarcoidosis manifests as noncaseating granulomas, predominantly in the lungs and intrathoracic lymph nodes. Approximately 5% of cases are asymptomatic and incidentally detected by chest radiography. Systemic complaints of fever, anorexia, and arthralgias occur in 45% of cases. Dyspnea on exertion, cough, chest pain, and hemoptysis (rare) occur in 50% of cases.

Lung hamartomas are the most common benign lung tumors, accounting for 75% of all benign lung tumors. About 80% are found in the peripheral portion of the lung. They are usually seen in males in the sixth decade. Hamartomas are made up of normal tissues such as cartilage, connective tissue, fat, and muscle but in abnormal amounts. Often there are no symptoms. More than 90% are found by accident, when a patient receives a chest X-ray or CT scan for some other reason.

70) A 55-year-old female patient had splenectomy for abdominal trauma due to RTA. A month after surgery, she was admitted with fever, cough and breathlessness. An organism was isolated in blood culture. What could be the probable organism?
   a. Staphylococcus
   b. E.coli
   c. Pneumococcus
   d. Klebsiella

Ans: (c)

Splenic injury can result from either blunt or penetrating chest or abdominal trauma; blunt mechanisms are more common. The spleen is one of the most commonly injured intra-abdominal organs. Emergent and urgent splenectomy is a life-saving measure for many patients.

Prevention of infection in patients with impaired splenic function

Patients with impaired splenic function are at risk for severe and overwhelming infections with encapsulated bacteria (eg, Streptococcus pneumoniae), bloodborne parasites, and other infections that the spleen plays an important role in controlling. Key measures for preventing such infections include patient education; vaccination against encapsulated bacteria and influenza; and use of prophylactic antibiotics.

Vaccinations - Advise all patients with impaired splenic function to receive vaccinations against S. pneumoniae (pneumococcus), H. influenzae type b, and N. meningitidis (meningococcus). For patients undergoing splenectomy, vaccines should be given ≥14 days prior to the procedure when feasible. When vaccines cannot be given in this time frame, they should be given 14 days after splenectomy.

Prophylactic antibiotics - In addition to vaccination, use of prophylactic antibiotics further reduces the risk of severe infections in patients with impaired splenic function. Provide all asplenic and hyposplenic patients with an emergency supply of antibiotics to be used in case of fever or other signs and symptoms of systemic infection (eg, chills, rigors, vomiting, or diarrhea) along with instruction to present to the nearest emergency department for additional care when such symptoms arise.

Penicillin and amoxicillin are the preferred agents for daily prophylaxis. Cephalosporins, fluoroquinolones, and macrolides are alternatives to penicillins.

For adults undergoing splenectomy, provide daily antibiotic prophylaxis for at least one year following the procedure.

For most children with anatomic or functional asplenia, daily antibiotic prophylaxis until age 5 and for at least one year following splenectomy is suggested. For children or adults with history of sepsis or other severe infections caused by an encapsulated organism (eg, S. pneumoniae), lifelong prophylaxis is suggested.

Animal bite - Advise patients with impaired splenic function to seek immediate medical care for any animal bite. Dog bites, in particular, can transmit Capnocytophaga canimorsus, which can be rapidly progressive and fatal in patients with impaired splenic function.

Pulmonary embolism

71) A 56-year-old patient, bed ridden for 2 months, suddenly develops breathlessness. CT scan of thorax is shown below. What is the diagnosis?

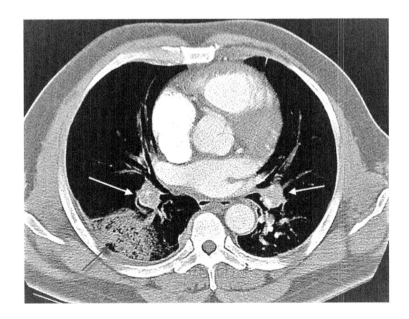

a. Aortic dissection
b. Pneumothorax

c. Pulmonary embolism

d. Pneumonia

Ans: (c)

Sudden onset of breathlessness in a bedridden patient indicates DVT and pulmonary embolism. For most patients with suspected PE, chest CT angiogram with contrast is the first-choice diagnostic imaging modality. See CT below

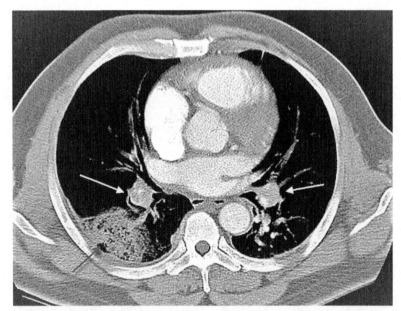

Axial CT scan of the chest shows bilateral filling defects in both pulmonary arteries (white arrows) representing thrombi. There is a large, wedge-shaped, pleural-based soft tissue density that represents the infarct and is called a Hampton Hump.

72) Modified Wells criteria

a. Pulmonary embolism

b. Pleural effusion

c. Cardiac tamponade

d. Myocardial infarction

Ans: (a)

Determining the pretest probability of pulmonary embolism

Whenever PE is suspected, the pretest probability (PTP) for PE should be estimated by clinical assessment or calculated using a validated PTP score (eg, Wells score, Modified Wells score, or Modified Geneva score).

Wells criteria

- Clinical symptoms of deep vein thrombosis (DVT) (3 points)
- Other diagnoses are less likely than PE (3 points)
- Heart rate >100 (1.5 points)
- Immobilization three or more days or surgery in previous four weeks (1.5 points)
- Previous DVT/PE (1.5 points)
- Hemoptysis (1 point)
- Malignancy (1 point)

The modified Wells score contains all the components of the original Wells score, with one additional point given to those with a history of previously documented DVT. The modified score classifies patients according to whether DVT is likely (a score of two or greater) or unlikely (a score of one or less).

73) A patient underwent pelvic surgery. A thrombus in which vein is most prone to cause pulmonary embolism?
   a. Iliac vein
   b. Femoral vein
   c. Calf vein
   d. Inferior vena cava

   Ans: (a)

90% of PE cases originate from the deep veins of the lower extremities and/or the pelvis. Venous thromboembolism is a leading cause of disability and death in postoperative hospitalized gynecologic patients. Without thromboprophylaxis, patients who undergo major gynecologic surgery have a prevalence of DVT in the range of 15%-40%.

74) A 40-year-old female came to emergency with acute onset of breathlessness after an air travel of 14 hours duration. The pulse rate is 120/min, BP is 140/80 mmHg and SO^2 is 80%. Bedside echo shows right ventricular dilatation with interventricular septum deviated to left. What is the management?
   a. Intravenous plasminogen activator
   b. Intravenous unfractionated heparin
   c. Embolectomy
   d. IVC filter

Ans: (b) Diagnosis is DVT of leg veins and pulmonary embolism. Pulmonary embolism is a complication of venous thromboembolism. Pulmonary emboli most commonly arise from thrombi that originate in the deep venous system of the lower extremities. The classic presentation of pulmonary embolism is the abrupt onset of pleuritic chest pain, shortness of breath, and hypoxia. The "classic" presentation is rarely seen.

The presence of right ventricular dilatation on bedside echocardiography has a sensitivity of 50% and specificity of 98% for the diagnosis of pulmonary embolism. Multidetector-row CT angiography (MDCTA) is the criterion standard for diagnosing pulmonary embolism.

Immediate full anticoagulation is mandatory for all patients suspected of having DVT or pulmonary embolism. Low-molecular-weight heparin (LMWH) is recommended for most patients with acute PE. Diagnostic investigations should not delay empirical anticoagulant therapy.

The currently accepted indications for thrombolytic therapy include hemodynamic instability (systolic BP <90 mm Hg) or a clinical risk factor assessment that suggests that hypotension is likely to develop. Thrombolytic therapy is not recommended for most patients with acute PE not associated with hypotension. Thrombolytic agents used in managing pulmonary embolism include alteplase, reteplase, urokinase and streptokinase.

Catheter embolectomy and fragmentation or surgical embolectomy is reasonable for patients with massive pulmonary embolism who have contraindications to fibrinolysis or who remain unstable after receiving fibrinolysis. These interventions are not recommended for patients with low-risk or submassive acute pulmonary embolism.

IVC filter is only indicated in the following settings:
- Patients with acute venous thromboembolism who have an absolute contraindication to anticoagulant therapy (eg, recent surgery, hemorrhagic stroke, significant active or recent bleeding)

- Patients with massive PE who survived but in whom recurrent embolism invariably will be fatal
- Patients who have recurrent venous thromboembolism, adequate anticoagulant therapy notwithstanding

Pleural disease

75) Transudative pleural effusion occurs in: (Multiple correct answers)
   a. Urinothorax
   b. Dressler syndrome
   c. Nephrotic syndrome
   d. Myxoedema
   e. Congestive heart failure

Ans: (a, c, d, e)

Pleural effusions are generally classified as transudates or exudates, based on the mechanism of fluid formation and pleural fluid chemistry. Transudates result from an imbalance in oncotic and hydrostatic pressures, whereas exudates are the result of inflammation of the pleura or decreased lymphatic drainage. In some cases, the pleural fluid may have a combination of transudative and exudative characteristics.

Light's Criteria

Fluid is exudate if one of the following Light's criteria is present:
1. Effusion protein/serum protein ratio greater than 0.5
2. Effusion LDH/serum LDH ratio greater than 0.6
3. Effusion LDH level greater than two-thirds the upper limit of the laboratory's reference range of serum LDH

Post-MI syndrome (Dressler syndrome)

Dressler syndrome is late pericardial inflammation occurring 2 weeks to 3 months after MI. It is an autoimmune process. Dressler syndrome is often associated with large *serosanguinous exudative* pleural and pericardial effusions.

Myxedema

Myxoedema is a severe form of hypothyroidism, usually applied to cases in which deposition of mucinous substances results in thickening of the skin and subcutaneous tissues. Pleural effusion is a rare manifestation. It may be a transudate or an exudate. Pleural effusions most commonly have been associated with ascites, pericardial fluid and heart failure. Most of these effusions respond to thyroid replacement therapy.

76) A patient with chest trauma has respiratory rate of 50/minute, BP of 90/60mmHg and hyperresonant note on the right chest. What is the next step?
   a. Incubate
   b. CXR
   c. IVF
   d. Wide bore needle insertion in second right intercostal space

Ans: (d) Hyperresonance on right hemithorax with tachypnea and hypotension indicate tension pneumothorax on the right side.

Tension pneumothorax

Gas in the pleural space is termed a pneumothorax. A tension pneumothorax is a life-threatening condition that develops when air is trapped in the pleural cavity under positive pressure, displacing mediastinal structures and compromising cardiopulmonary function. Tension pneumothorax is a clinical diagnosis based on patient presentation. Respiratory distress and chest pain are universally present, and tachycardia and ipsilateral air entry on auscultation are also common findings.

Suspicion of tension pneumothorax mandates immediate treatment and does not require potentially prolonged diagnostic studies. A large-bore needle should be inserted into the pleural space through the second anterior intercostal space. If large amounts of gas escape from the needle after insertion, the diagnosis is confirmed. The needle should be left in place until a thoracostomy tube can be inserted.

For patients with suspected pneumothorax who are hemodynamically unstable or in severe respiratory distress, recommended action is rapid bedside imaging with pleural ultrasonography, if available, with ongoing resuscitation efforts focused on stabilizing the airway, breathing, and circulation. Ultrasonography has high sensitivity (96%), specificity (100%), and diagnostic effectiveness (99%) for pneumothorax. If ultrasonography is unavailable or unhelpful, then an empiric decision to place a chest tube without confirmatory imaging should be made on clinical assessment alone.

For most stable patients with suspected pneumothorax, bedside chest radiography in the upright position is suggested.

Chest CT is the most accurate method available for detection of pneumothorax.

77) A 40-year-female met with a road traffic accident. On examination GCS is 15/15, heart rate is 160 bpm and BP is 100/60 mm Hg. JVP is elevated. Chest is tympanic on percussion

with decreased breath sounds. Ecchymosis are present over chest and is abdomen is soft. What is the diagnosis?
a. Cardiac tamponade
b. Tension pneumothorax
c. Massive hemothorax
d. Pericardial effusion

Ans: (b)

The combination of tympanic chest on percussion, decreased breath sounds and raised JVP in a trauma patient suggests tension pneumothorax. Pneumothorax is a common complication of chest trauma, often sustained from a fractured rib. Patients may manifest tachypnea, chest pain, hypoxia, unilateral diminished or absent breath sounds, or unilateral hyperresonance to percussion, depending upon the extent of the pneumothorax. The supine chest radiograph has high specificity for diagnosing a pneumothorax from blunt injury, but its sensitivity is variable. Ultrasound may be a more sensitive initial screening tool.

Cardiac tamponade is characterized by the accumulation of pericardial fluid under pressure. Acute cardiac tamponade is sudden in onset, may be associated with chest pain, tachypnea, and dyspnea, and is life-threatening if not promptly treated. The jugular venous pressure is markedly elevated and may be associated with venous distension in the forehead and scalp. The heart sounds are often muted. Hypotension is common due to the decline in cardiac output. Pulsus paradoxus, defined as an abnormally large decrease in systolic blood pressure (>10 mmHg) on inspiration, is a common finding in moderate to severe cardiac tamponade.

78) A patient has a silent resonant hemithorax on examination. What is the diagnosis?
a. Large pleural effusion
b. Pneumothorax
c. Bronchial asthma

d. Consolidation

Ans: (b)

Characteristic physical findings when a large pneumothorax is present include decreased chest excursion on the affected side, diminished breath sounds, and hyperresonant percussion. Subcutaneous emphysema may be present. Evidence of labored breathing and hemodynamic compromise (eg, tachycardia, hypotension) suggests a possible tension pneumothorax, which necessitates emergency decompression.

Pleural effusion and consolidation cause dull percussion note.

Bronchial asthma may cause bilateral resonant silent chest.

79) A 16-year-old tall and thin built patient came to the emergency with hypotension and severe dyspnea. On examination, trachea was deviated to right side. Percussion note was hyperresonant on left hemithorax with absent breath sounds. What is the management?
  a. Send the patient to urgent x-ray
  b. Put the patient on positive pressure ventilation for hypoxia
  c. Emergency chest decompression with needle thoracotomy
  d. Start vasopressors for low BP

Ans: (c)

Diagnosis is left tension pneumothorax (hyperresonance on left hemithorax with absent breath sounds, hypotension and severe dyspnea) in a patient with Marfan syndrome (tall and thin built).

A large-bore needle should be inserted into the pleural space through the second anterior intercostal space. If large amounts of gas escape from the needle after insertion, the diagnosis is confirmed. The needle should be left in place until a thoracostomy tube can be inserted.

Tension pneumothorax

Pneumothorax is the presence of air or gas in the pleural cavity. Tension pneumothorax is most common in patients with traumatic pneumothorax.

Pathophysiology

Tension pneumothorax develops when injured tissue forms a 1-way valve, allowing air inflow with inhalation into the pleural space and prohibiting air outflow. The volume of this intrapleural air increases with each inspiration because of the 1-way valve effect. As a result, pressure rises within the affected hemithorax. As the pressure increases, the ipsilateral lung collapses and causes hypoxia. Further pressure increases cause the mediastinum to shift toward the contralateral side; result is compression of the contralateral lung and impaired venous return to the right atrium due to compression of the thin walls of the atria and kinking of the inferior vena cava. Hypoxia results as the collapsed lung on the affected side and the compressed lung on the contralateral side compromise effective gas exchange. This hypoxia and decreased venous return caused by compression of the relatively thin walls of the atria impair cardiac function.

Treatment

Tension pneumothorax rapidly progresses to respiratory insufficiency, cardiovascular collapse, and, ultimately, death if not recognized and treated. Therefore, if the clinical picture fits a tension pneumothorax, it must be emergently treated before it results in hemodynamic instability and death. Prompt recognition of this condition is lifesaving.

Immediate decompression of the thorax is mandatory when tension pneumothorax is suspected. This should not be delayed for radiographic confirmation.

Immediate needle decompression

Treatment of tension pneumothorax is emergent and should be performed before confirmatory radiologic studies. If a tension pneumothorax is suspected, immediate needle decompression is indicated. Needle decompression is performed before definitive treatment with tube thoracostomy.

A large-bore IV needle should be inserted into the pleural space through the second anterior intercostal space. If large amounts of gas escape from the needle after insertion, the diagnosis is confirmed. This procedure converts the tension pneumothorax into an open pneumothorax. The needle should be left in place until a thoracostomy tube can be inserted.

Tube thoracostomy

Once the tension pneumothorax is decompressed the patient's perfusion often improves immediately. A needle decompression is a temporary measure only and should be followed promptly by the insertion of a large-bore chest tube (tube thoracostomy) on the side of the tension pneumothorax. Place tube thoracostomy decompression tube in the second rib interspace in the midclavicular line. A midclavicular approach is very important because the internal mammary vessels are located approximately 3 cm away from the sternal border. Place the catheter just above the cephalad border of the rib, because the intercostal vessels are largest on the lower edge of the rib.

80) Structure not pierced during pleural tap
   a. Intercostal muscle
   b. Parietal pleura
   c. Visceral pleura
   d. Skin

Ans: (c)

The visceral pleura is the delicate serous membrane that covers the surface of each lung and dips into the fissures between the lobes. The parietal pleura is the outer membrane, which is attached to the inner surface of the thoracic cavity. Pleural fluid collects in the space between the parietal and visceral pleurae. See the figure below.

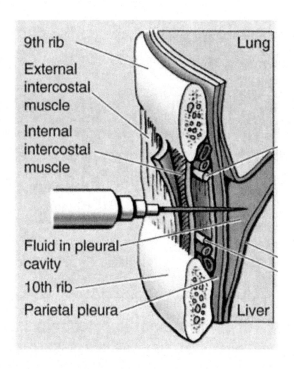

81) Not a feature of pleural effusion associated with rheumatoid arthritis -
   a. RA factor positive
   b. High glucose
   c. Cholesterol crystals
   d. High LDH

Ans: (b)

In rheumatoid effusions, pleural fluid analysis typically reveals a white cell count <5000/mm3, a pleural fluid glucose <60 mg/dL or a pleural fluid to serum glucose ratio less than 0.5, a pH less than 7.3, and high pleural fluid LDH level (ie, greater than 700 IU/L).

Less commonly, patients with RA and a long-standing pleural effusion may have a cholesterol effusion (also known as a pseudochylous or chyliform effusion). Cholesterol effusions have the milky or opaque appearance of an empyema but are sterile. The milky appearance is due to an elevated cholesterol level (above 200 mg/dL and sometimes

106

over 1000 mg/dL); cholesterol crystals, identifiable with polarized light, may also be present.

Empyema due to infection has similar pleural fluid chemistries to a rheumatoid effusion (ie, exudative, low pH, low glucose); the possibility of infection needs to be fully evaluated with bacterial and mycobacterial stains and culture, particularly in patients taking glucocorticoids.

82) Most common pulmonary manifestation of SLE
   a. Shrinking Lung
   b. Pleuritis
   c. Intra alveolar haemorrhage
   d. Interstitial inflammation

Ans: (b)

Most patients with SLE develop involvement of the lung, its vasculature, the pleura, and/or the diaphragm at some time during their course. Pleurisy, coughing, and/or dyspnea are often the first clues.

Patients with SLE and lung involvement must always be evaluated for infection, particularly due to bacteria or viruses. Many patients with SLE are immunocompromised due to the underlying disease or ongoing medications; therefore, opportunistic infections (eg, mycobacteria or fungi) should also be considered.

Sarcoidosis

83) False about sarcoidosis:
   a. High CD4: CD8 ratio
   b. Hypercalciuria and hypercalcemia may be present
   c. Increased serum levels of angiotensin-converting enzyme
   d. Schaumann and asteroid bodies are pathognomonic

Ans: (d)

Sarcoidosis is a multisystem inflammatory disease of unknown etiology that manifests as noncaseating granulomas, predominantly in the lungs and intrathoracic lymph nodes. The lungs are affected in approximately 90 percent of patients. Other tissues commonly involved include the skin, eyes, and lymph nodes.

CD4/CD8 ratio

T cells play a central role in the development of sarcoidosis. The initial lesion within the pulmonary system is a CD4+ T cell alveolitis, followed by the development of noncaseating granulomata.

There are 2 major phenotypes of circulating mature T lymphocytes. One type expresses the cluster determinant 4 (abbreviated as "CD4") on its surface and they are generally associated with helper/inducer function (helper T lymphocytes). The other type expresses the cluster determinant 8 (abbreviated as "CD8") and they are usually associated with cytotoxic/suppressor activity (cytotoxic T cells).

The CD4 and CD8 molecules mediate adhesion to major histocompatibility complex class II and class I molecules, respectively. In addition, CD4 and CD8 amplify stimulatory signals through the T cell receptor.

A CD4:CD8 ratio is calculated by dividing the number of CD4+ T cells by the number of CD8+ T cells. A normal CD4/CD8 ratio is about 2.0 (1.5 to 2.5). This means that there are about 1 to 2 CD4 cells for every CD8 cell. Evaluation of the CD4/CD8 ratio is routine in HIV infection. In HIV infection, the CD4:CD8 ratio is usually less than 1. This reflects increasing numbers of CD8+ T cells and depletion of CD4+ T cells in chronic infection.

Patients with pulmonary sarcoidosis frequently have increased numbers of lymphocytes and a high ratio of CD4+ to CD8+ T-lymphocytes (CD4/CD8 ratio) in bronchoalveolar lavage (BAL) fluid. However, CD4/CD8 ratio in BAL fluid is highly variable. Pulmonary sarcoidosis is frequently characterized by a CD4+/CD8+ ratio of at least

3.5 in bronchoalveolar lavage fluid, although up to 40% of the cases present a normal or even decreased ratio, thus limiting its diagnostic value.

Abnormal calcium homeostasis

Approximately 30 to 50 percent of patients with sarcoidosis have hypercalciuria, and 10 to 20 percent have hypercalcemia, which is aggravated by exposure to sunlight. Activated pulmonary macrophages in sarcoidosis produce calcitriol, the active form of vitamin D. Calcitriol is responsible for the hypercalciuria and hypercalcemia that are frequently seen. Increased intestinal calcium absorption induced by high serum calcitriol concentrations (1,25-dihydroxyvitamin D, the most active metabolite of vitamin D) is the primary abnormality, although a calcitriol-induced increase in bone resorption may also contribute.

ACE levels

Serum ACE levels are elevated in 60% of patients at the time of diagnosis. Non-caseating granulomas secrete ACE, which may function as a cytokine. Serum ACE levels may correlate with total body granuloma load. Levels may be increased in fluid from bronchoalveolar lavage or in cerebrospinal fluid.

Sensitivity and specificity as a diagnostic test is limited (60% and 70%, respectively). Elevated serum levels of angiotensin-converting enzyme may also be associated with a wide variety of other disorders, including tuberculosis, leprosy, primary biliary cirrhosis, diabetes mellitus, pulmonary neoplasm, lymphoma, Gaucher disease, and hyperthyroidism.

There is no clear prognostic value. Serum ACE levels may decline in response to therapy. Decisions on treatment should not be based on the ACE level alone.

The pathologic hallmark of sarcoidosis is the presence of discrete, noncaseating, epithelioid cell granulomas. The dominant cell in the central core is the epithelioid cell (differentiated mononuclear phagocyte). Granulomas may contain cytoplasmic inclusion bodies including Schaumann bodies (concentrically calcified bodies), asteroid bodies (eosinophilic, star-shaped inclusions), and Hamazaki–Wesenberg bodies. See figures below. These are not specific for sarcoidosis. A variety of inclusion bodies, such as asteroid bodies and Schaumann bodies may be found within the cytoplasm of giant cells of different granulomas (infections, berylliosis, Crohn disease, and local "sarcoid reactions" that occur near neoplastic, foreign body, or chronic inflammatory areas).

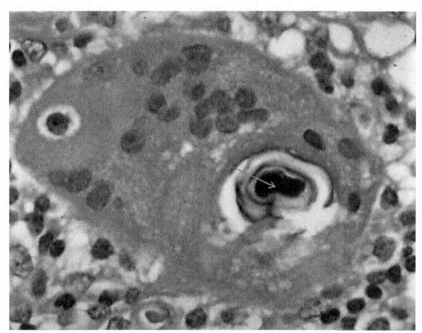

Arrow - Schaumann bodies

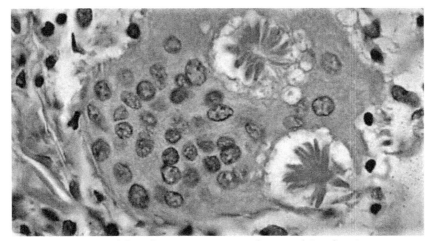

Asteroid bodies are star-shaped inclusions

84) Which is not a feature of Lofgren syndrome?
   a. Vasculitis
   b. Erythema nodosum
   c. Polyarthralgia
   d. Bilateral hilar adenopathy

Ans: (a)

Lofgren syndrome is the combination of erythema nodosum (EN), hilar adenopathy, migratory polyarthralgia, and uveitis seen primarily in women. Men with acute sarcoidosis may present with signs of bilateral ankle arthritis typical of Lofgren syndrome, but without EN. The presence of all features of the Lofgren syndrome has a 95 percent diagnostic specificity for sarcoidosis, allowing a clinical diagnosis to be made without biopsy. Lofgren syndrome is associated with a good prognosis and spontaneous remission. Treatment with NSAIDs is usually adequate to control symptoms.

Radiology

85) What do the arrows show?

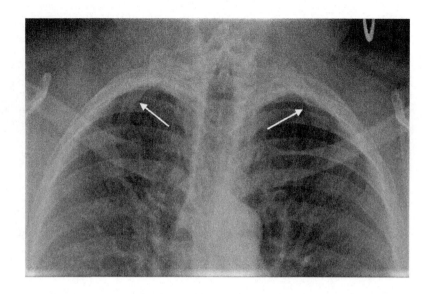

a. Normal first rib
b. Normal second rib
c. First rib fracture
d. First rib myeloma
e. Cervical rib

Ans: (e)

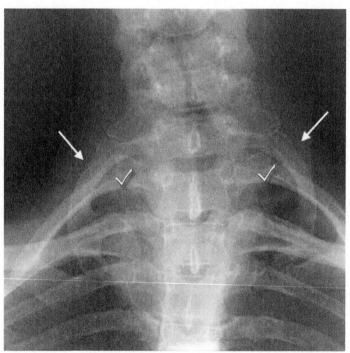

Bilateral cervical ribs arising from the 7th cervical vertebral body (white arrows). The check marks show the normal, first ribs.

Cervical Rib

General Considerations

- Rare anomaly, occurring in just 1% of population
- The rib or ribs arise from the 7th cervical vertebral body
- They are usually bilateral (80%)
- More common in females
- The anterior end of the cervical rib may attach to the first rib, the sternum, or the cartilage of the first rib; it may be a fibrous band, or it may have no anterior attachment

Clinical Findings

- Most are asymptomatic
- Less than 10% of those with cervical ribs will be symptomatic
- Their clinical importance is their association with thoracic outlet syndrome

Neurogenic Thoracic Outlet Syndrome

- Most common form of thoracic outlet syndrome
- Caused by compression of the lower portion of the brachial plexus
- Clinical manifestations may include pain in the neck and shoulder which radiates into the upper extremity affecting course of the ulnar nerve-hand and inner forearm
- Hand weakness, numbness, and clumsiness

Arterial thoracic outlet syndrome (least common)

- Most serious form of the syndrome
- Men and women affected equally
- Digital vasospasm, potential thrombosis or embolism, aneurysm, muscle atrophy, and gangrene

Venous thoracic outlet syndrome

- Young men are most often affected
- Characterized by arm claudication, edema, cyanosis, and venous dilatation
- Results from the compression of the subclavian vein

Treatment

Most patients improve with exercise and physical therapy. Indications for surgical resection of the accessory rib may include disabling pain, paresthesias and failure of conservative treatment

86) A 50-year-old male has presented with dyspnea, restlessness and tachypnea. The chest X-ray is shown below. What is the diagnosis?

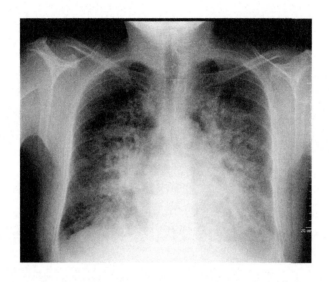

    a. Pulmonary edema
    b. Pulmonary embolism
    c. Lymphangitis carcinomatosis
    d. Lung collapse

Ans: (a)

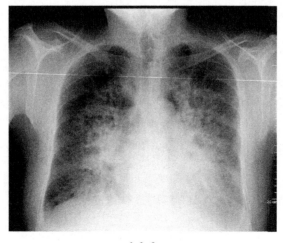

Bilateral perihilar alveolar edema give the typical "butterfly" appearance

X-ray shows symmetrical area of shadowing in the central region of both lungs, heart enlargement with congestion in the pulmonary veins and bilateral small pleural effusions. These findings are typical of cardiac failure and pulmonary edema.

Prominence of the upper zone veins is the earliest abnormality noted in the chest X-ray in chronic LVF. This is due to pulmonary venous hypertension. This corresponds to a pulmonary capillary pressure of about 18 - 20 Hg. Dyspnea and mild tachypnea is commonly present.

Kerley B lines correspond to a pulmonary capillary pressure of about 20 to 25 mm Hg. Kerley B lines are due to interstitial edema. Dyspnea and tachypnea increases.

Bat – wing or Butterfly appearance finally appear in the x-ray chest corresponding to a pulmonary capillary pressure more than 25 mm Hg. See x-ray picture above. At this advanced stage of pulmonary edema, bilateral basal crepitations and rhonchi are usually audible. Typically, the patient is anxious and sweating profusely. The sputum is frothy, and blood tinged.

When pulmonary capillary pressure exceeds 25 mm Hg, pleural effusions may occur. Pleural effusions are common in patients with chronic heart failure. Ultrasonography is better than x-ray to detect pleural effusion (and pericardial effusion).

87) Elevation of hemidiaphragm
    a. Pulmonary hypoplasia
    b. Subphrenic infection
    c. Phrenic nerve palsy
    d. All the above

Ans: (d)

The right hemi-diaphragm usually lies at a level slightly above the left. There are many possible causes of a raised hemidiaphragm such as damage to the phrenic nerve, lung disease causing volume loss, congenital causes such as a diaphragmatic hernia, or trauma to the diaphragm. See table below.

Causes of elevated hemidiaphragm

Above the diaphragm
- Decreased lung volume
- Atelectasis/collapse
- Lobectomy/pneumonectomy
- Pulmonary hypoplasia

Diaphragm
- Phrenic nerve palsy
- Diaphragmatic eventration
- Contralateral stroke: usually middle cerebral artery distribution

Below the diaphragm
- Abdominal tumour, e.g. liver metastases or primary malignancy
- Subphrenic abscess
- Distended stomach or colon

88) A patient developed respiratory distress following dog bite over the left side of neck. Chest x-ray is shown below. What is the diagnosis?

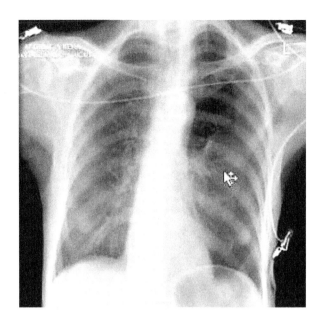

a. Pneumothorax
b. Subcutaneous emphysema
c. Pneumomediastinum
d. Pneumoperitoneum

Ans: (a)

X-ray shows absence of bronchovascular markings in the left upper zone.

89) A child presented to hospital 12hrs after dog bite on neck. X-ray is shown below. What is the diagnosis?

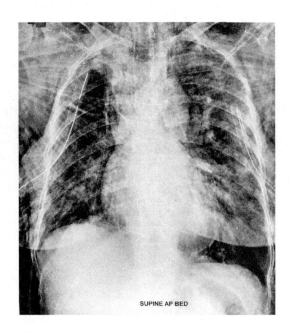

SUPINE AP BED

    a. Subcutaneous emphysema

    b. Bilateral Pneumothorax

    c. Pneumoperitoneum

    d. Injury to carotids

Ans: (a)

Subcutaneous or surgical emphysema refers to air in the subcutaneous tissues. This usually occurs in the chest, face or neck. Clinically it is felt as crepitus and, if extensive, may cause soft tissue swelling. Trauma is the most common cause. Plain radiograph shows lucencies in the soft tissues. Even when severe subcutaneous emphysema is typically benign. The subcutaneous air is absorbed by the body over time.

90) Commonly present in middle mediastinum
    a. Schwannoma
    b. Thymoma
    c. Bronchogenic cyst
    d. Teratoma
    e. Substernal thyroid
Ans: (c)

The mediastinum is the partition between the lungs. It includes the mediastinal pleura, although it is commonly applied to the region between the two pleural sacs. It is bounded anteriorly by the sternum and posteriorly by the thoracic vertebral column. It extends vertically from the thoracic inlet to the diaphragm. It is divided into a superior and an inferior mediastinum. The inferior mediastinum is subdivided into anterior, middle and posterior parts. The division into upper and lower mediastina is by an imaginary line from the manubriosternal joint and the lower surface of the fourth thoracic vertebra. Superior mediastinum lies between the manubrium sterni and the upper four thoracic vertebrae.

The Three Compartments of the Mediastinum

	Anterior Compartment	Middle Compartment	Posterior Compartment
Anatomical boundaries	Manubrium and sternum anteriorly, pericardium, aorta, and brachiocephalic vessels posteriorly	Anterior mediastinum anteriorly, posterior mediastinum posteriorly	Pericardium and trachea anteriorly; vertebral column posteriorly
Contents	Thymus gland, anterior mediastinal lymph nodes, internal mammary arteries and veins	Pericardium, heart, ascending and transverse arch of aorta, superior and inferior vena cavae, brachiocephalic arteries and veins, phrenic nerves, trachea, and main	Descending thoracic aorta, esophagus, thoracic duct, azygos and hemiazygos veins, sympathetic chains, and the posterior group of mediastinal lymph nodes

		bronchi and their contiguous lymph nodes, pulmonary arteries, and veins	
Common causes	Thymoma, lymphomas, teratomatous neoplasms, thyroid masses, parathyroid masses, mesenchymal tumors, giant lymph node hyperplasia, hernia through foramen of Morgagni	Metastatic lymph node enlargement, granulomatous lymph node enlargement, pleuropericardial cysts, bronchogenic cysts, masses of vascular origin	Neurogenic tumors, meningocele, meningomyelocele, gastroenteric cysts, esophageal diverticula, hernia through foramen of Bochdalek, extramedullary hematopoiesis

91) Tumor that does not present in the anterior mediastinum -
   a. Lymphoma
   b. Thymoma
   c. Neurogenic tumors
   d. Thyroid mass

   Ans: (c)

The mediastinum is the partition between the lungs. It includes the mediastinal pleura, although it is commonly applied to the region between the two pleural sacs. It is bounded anteriorly by the sternum and posteriorly by the thoracic vertebral column. It extends vertically from the thoracic inlet to the diaphragm. It is divided into a superior and an inferior mediastinum. The inferior mediastinum is subdivided into anterior, middle, and posterior parts. The division into upper and lower mediastina is by an imaginary line from the manubriosternal joint and the lower surface of the fourth thoracic vertebra. Superior mediastinum lies between the manubrium sterni and the upper four thoracic vertebrae. See figure below.

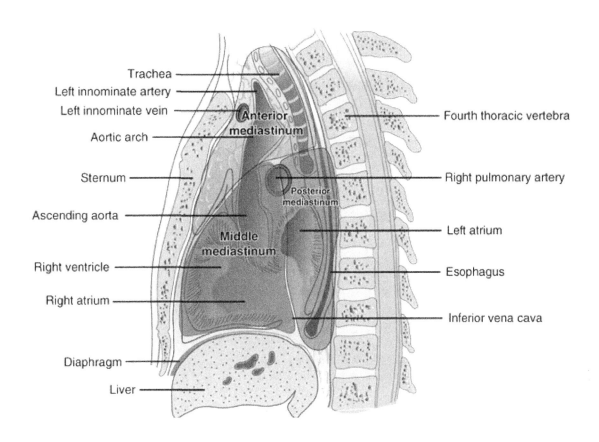

	Anterior Compartment	Middle Compartment	Posterior Compartment
Anatomical boundaries	Manubrium and sternum anteriorly, pericardium, aorta, and brachiocephalic vessels posteriorly	Anterior mediastinum anteriorly, posterior mediastinum posteriorly	Pericardium and trachea anteriorly; vertebral column posteriorly
Contents	Thymus gland, anterior mediastinal lymph nodes, internal mammary arteries, and veins	Pericardium, heart, ascending and transverse arch of aorta, superior and inferior vena cavae, brachiocephalic arteries and veins, phrenic nerves, trachea, and main bronchi and their contiguous lymph nodes, pulmonary arteries, and veins	Descending thoracic aorta, esophagus, thoracic duct, azygos and hemiazygos veins, sympathetic chains, and the posterior group of mediastinal lymph nodes
Common abnormalitie	Thymoma, lymphomas,	Metastatic lymph node	Neurogenic tumors,

s	teratomatous neoplasms, thyroid masses, parathyroid masses, mesenchymal tumors, giant lymph node hyperplasia, hernia through foramen of Morgagni	enlargement, granulomatous lymph node enlargement, pleuropericardial cysts, bronchogenic cysts, masses of vascular origin	meningocele, meningomyelocele, gastroenteric cysts, esophageal diverticula, hernia through foramen of Bochdalek, extramedullary hematopoiesis

92) A 34-year-old male patient has presented with dyspnoea and productive cough with postural variation. The patient has been a heavy smoker for 20 years. The patient also has a history of recent binge drinking. The chest X-ray taken is shown below. What is the management?

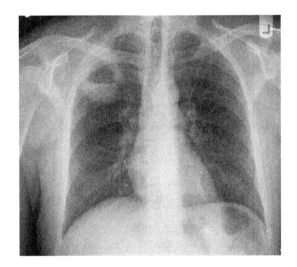

   a. Gemcitabine and carboplatin-based chemotherapy
   b. Lobectomy
   c. Intravenous clindamycin and fluids
   d. Antituberculous therapy

Ans: (c) The x-ray shows a lung abscess in the right upper zone, most likely caused by aspiration pneumonia.

Aspiration pneumonia is caused by aspirated oropharyngeal flora. Aspiration pneumonia is caused by bacteria that normally reside in the oral and nasal pharynx. Anaerobic species are the most common organisms. Anaerobes are common constituents of the normal flora in a susceptible host prone to aspiration.

Conditions that alter consciousness and periodontal disease specifically predispose the patient to bacterial pneumonia. Almost all patients who develop aspiration pneumonia have one or more of the predisposing conditions listed below.

- Alcoholism
- Drug overdose
- Seizures
- Stroke
- Head trauma
- General anaesthesia
- Intracranial mass lesion

The right lower lung lobe is the most common site of infiltrate formation due to the larger calibre and more vertical orientation of the right main stem bronchus. The right upper lobe may be involved particularly in alcoholics who aspirate while in the prone position. Chest radiographic findings in patients with anaerobic bacterial pneumonia typically demonstrate an infiltrate with or without cavitation in one of the dependent segments of the lungs (i.e., posterior segments of the upper lobes, superior segments of the lower lobes). Air-fluid levels within a circumscribed infiltrate indicate a lung abscess.

Antibiotics are the most important component of treatment of aspiration pneumonia due to bacterial infection. When anaerobic bacteria are probable pathogens in aspiration pneumonia, ampicillin-sulbactam may be given. Alternative agents are the combination of metronidazole plus either amoxicillin or penicillin G.

Clindamycin is no longer favoured because of high levels of resistance to beta-lactams and the risk of C. difficile infection. Clindamycin is an appropriate choice for penicillin-allergic patients.

93) A 55-year-old non-smoker has presented with hemoptysis, productive cough with large amounts of sputum and clubbing. There is no fever. The chest X-ray is shown below. What is the diagnosis?

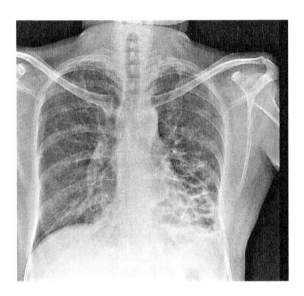

    a. Interstitial lung disease
    b. Bronchiectasis
    c. Lung carcinoma
    d. Pulmonary edema

Ans: (b) The combination of productive cough with large amounts of sputum, clubbing and hemoptysis suggests bronchiectasis.

Bronchiectasis

Bronchiectasis is irreversible, abnormal dilatation of the bronchi. The dilated bronchi are inflamed and easily collapsible, resulting in airflow obstruction and impaired clearance of secretions. Bronchiectasis typically presents with cough, sputum production, and airway obstruction, and in severe cases, massive hemoptysis that can lead to death.

Volumetric multidetector CT

Diagnosis of bronchiectasis is based on a clinical history of daily viscid sputum production and characteristic CT scan findings. High-resolution computed tomography (HRCT) scanning was once the imaging modality of choice for assessing suspected bronchiectasis. Volumetric multidetector CT acquisition of the chest is now the preferred examination for the diagnosis of bronchiectasis.

Chest x-rays

Chest x-rays are usually abnormal but are inadequate in the diagnosis or quantification of bronchiectasis. The chest x-ray may show the presence of increased pulmonary markings, ring-like structures, atelectasis, dilated and thickened airways (tram lines), and mucus plugging (finger-in-glove) appearance; however, the chest radiograph may be normal even in the presence of bronchiectasis.

94) Enlarged bilateral hilar lymph nodes with eggshell calcification in a chest radiograph
    a. Sarcoidosis
    b. Asbestosis
    c. Silicosis
    d. Anthracosis

Ans: (c)

Eggshell calcification refers to fine calcification seen at the periphery of an enlarged lymph node. See x-ray below.

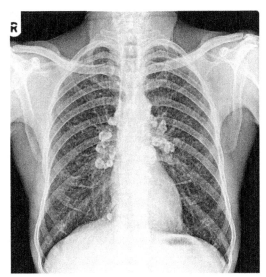

Plain X-ray posteroanterior view showing bilateral hilar adenopathy with eggshell calcification.

Eggshell calcification is most commonly seen in occupational diseases, like silicosis and coal-worker's pneumoconiosis as well as sarcoidosis but rarely in post-irradiated Hodgkin's disease, blastomycosis, scleroderma, amyloid and histoplasmosis.

Silicosis is a fibronodular lung disease caused by inhalation of dust containing crystalline silica (alpha-quartz or silicon dioxide). Calcification of the hilar lymph nodes, particularly in the rim of the nodes (ie, eggshell calcification) is very characteristic of silicosis. However, eggshell calcifications are observed only in a minority of cases of silicosis.

95) Hilar lymph node calcification in a CT scan: (Multiple correct answers)
   a. Asbestosis
   b. Silicosis
   c. Amyloidosis
   d. Berylliosis
   e. Coal worker pneumoconiosis

Ans: (b, d & e)

- Infectious granulomatous diseases
  - o Tuberculosis
  - o Histoplasmosis
- Sarcoidosis
- Silicosis
- Coal-worker's pneumoconiosis
- Rarely in post-irradiated Hodgkin disease, blastomycosis, scleroderma, amyloid and histoplasmosis

96) Comet tail sign on CT is seen in:
   a. Round atelectasis
   b. Round pneumonia
   c. Bronchopneumonia
   d. Lobar pneumonia

   Ans: (a)

Rounded atelectasis is a rare form of peripheral alveolar collapse that develops as a result of pleural diseases. The lesion is always adherent to the surface of the pleura and may suggest a carcinoma of the lung. The most common cause of rounded atelectasis is occupational exposure to mineral dusts: asbestosis, pneumoconiosis, inhalation of mixed mineral dusts. A history of asbestos exposure is present in 70% of cases.   Round atelectasis is almost always asymptomatic and is detected on chest radiographs obtained for other reasons. The characteristic feature of round atelectasis is the comet tail sign.

Comet tail sign
The comet tail sign is seen on computed tomographic scans of the chest in round atelectasis. It consists of a curvilinear opacity that extends from a subpleural "mass" toward the ipsilateral hilum. The comet tail sign is produced by the distortion of vessels and bronchi

that lead to an adjacent area of round atelectasis, which is the mass. The bronchovascular bundles appear to be pulled into the mass and resemble a comet tail.

As the lung collapses, the vessels and bronchi that lead to the mass are pulled into the region. As they reach the mass, they diverge and arch around the undersurface to merge with the inferior pole of the mass. This characteristic distortion is well demonstrated at conventional tomography. See 2 figures below.

Comet tail

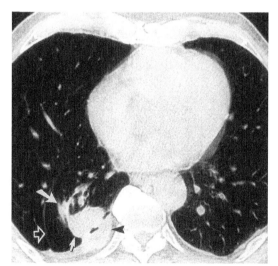

Round atelectasis in an asymptomatic 66-year-old man with a history of asbestos exposure. CT scan of the chest demonstrates a mass (short white arrow) in the right lower lobe of the lung. Bronchovascular bundles (long white arrow) converge into the mass in a curvilinear fashion. Pleural thickening (arrowhead) is present.

97) Massive hemoptysis seen in -
   a. Mitral stenosis
   b. Aortic stenosis
   c. Pulmonary stenosis
   d. Aortic regurgitation

   Ans: (a)

One definition of massive hemoptysis is either ≥500 mL of expectorated blood over a 24-hour period or bleeding at a rate ≥100 mL/hour, regardless of whether abnormal gas exchange or hemodynamic instability exists.

Mitral stenosis increases resistance in the pulmonary veins, accompanied by reversal of blood flow from the pulmonary capillaries into the bronchial veins. The resulting submucosal bronchial varices may rupture, causing "cardiac apoplexy." This is prone to manifest at times of either increased pulmonary blood flow (exercise, pregnancy) or increased blood volume (pregnancy).

98) A patient has presented with recurrent haemoptysis. Which vessels should be evaluated for angiography? (Multiple correct answers)
   a. Pulmonary artery
   b. Pulmonary vein
   c. Branchial artery
   d. Branchial vein
   e. Superior vena cava

   Ans: (a & c)

Blood traversing the lungs can arrive from one of two sources: pulmonary arteries or bronchial arteries.

One or two bronchial arteries supply each lung. They typically arise from the aorta and less commonly from the intercostal or vertebral arteries. These vessels provide the nutritive blood supply to the airways, hilar lymph nodes, visceral pleura, and some portions of the mediastinum.

The entire cardiac output passes through the high-pressure pulmonary arteries. In contrast, the bronchial arteries arise from systemic arteries and are under much higher systemic pressure but carry only a small portion of the cardiac output.

Bleeding from a bronchial artery is the cause of massive hemoptysis in 90 percent of cases. Despite the quantitatively smaller contribution of the bronchial circulation to pulmonary blood flow, the bronchial arteries are generally a more important source of hemoptysis than the pulmonary circulation. In some circumstances, such as bronchiectasis, the bronchial circulation becomes hyperplastic and tortuous, and can be a source of massive hemoptysis.

99) Cigarette smoking increases the risk of all the following diseases except -
   a. Pancreatic carcinoma
   b. Cerebrovascular accident
   c. Sudden infant death syndrome
   d. Primary pulmonary hypertension

   Ans: (d)

Cigarette smoking and exposure to tobacco smoke is the leading cause of premature, preventable death; about 36% are from cancer, 39% are from heart disease and stroke, and 24% are from lung disease.

Smoking increases the risk of at least 14 cancers, including cancer of the lung, larynx, oesophagus, mouth and pharynx, bladder, pancreas, kidney, liver, stomach, bowel, cervix, ovary, nose and sinuses, as well as some types of leukaemia. There is some evidence that smoking could cause breast cancer.

A pregnant smoker is at higher risk of miscarriage, having an ectopic pregnancy, having her baby born too early and with an abnormally low birth weight, and having her baby born with a cleft lip and/or cleft palate. A woman who smokes during or after pregnancy increases her infant's risk of death from sudden infant death syndrome (SIDS).

100) Caisson's disease is seen in –
   a. Cotton field agricultural workers
   b. Construction workers under sea level
   c. Workers in manufacture of gas
   d. Workers in radiation units

Ans: (b)

Decompression sickness (Caisson disease)
Barotrauma is the most common form of diving-related injury; it develops when an air-filled body space fails to equilibrate its pressure with the environment.

As a diver descends and breathes air under increased pressure, the tissues become loaded with increased quantities of oxygen and nitrogen. As the diver returns to the surface, gas tensions in the tissue exceed the ambient pressure, leading to the liberation of free gas from the tissues in the form of bubbles. The liberated gas bubbles can alter organ function by blocking vessels, rupturing, or compressing tissue, or activating clotting and inflammatory cascades. The volume and location of these bubbles determine if symptoms occur. 90 percent of patients with decompression sickness develop symptoms within 12 hours of surfacing.

101) Not used for smoking cessation
   a. Nicotine gum
   b. Clonazepam
   c. Bupropion
   d. Varenicline

Ans: (b)

Smokers should be managed with a combination of behavioral support and pharmacologic therapy. First-line pharmacologic therapies for smoking cessation include nicotine replacement therapy (NRT), varenicline, and bupropion.

102) Which of the following is not a component of syndrome Z?
   a. Obstructive sleep apnea
   b. Blood pressure more than 130/85mm Hg
   c. Fasting triglyceride more than 150mg/ dl
   d. LDL more than 100mg/dl

Ans: (d)

Syndrome Z

Syndrome Z is defined as the co-occurrence of obstructive sleep apnea (OSA) and metabolic syndrome. The metabolic syndrome (Syndrome X) is characterized by abdominal obesity, arterial hypertension, increased blood triglycerides, decreased high-density lipoprotein (HDL) cholesterol and increased blood glucose. Insulin resistance and an increased amount of abdominal fat may be the pathogenic factors responsible for the variety of symptoms of the metabolic syndrome.

Metabolic syndrome (Syndrome X)

- Central obesity as measured by waist circumference: In men greater than 40 inches and in women greater than 35 inches
- Fasting blood triglycerides greater than or equal to 150 mg/dL
- Blood HDL cholesterol: In men less than 40 mg/dL, and in women less than 50 mg/dL
- Blood pressure greater than or equal to 130/85 mmHg
- Fasting blood glucose greater than or equal to 110 mg/dL

OSA is characterized by recurrent partial or complete collapse of the upper airway in the presence of ventilatory effort during sleep. These events are often associated with recurrent nocturnal oxyhemoglobin desaturation, fragmented sleep, major fluctuations in blood pressure, and increased sympathetic nervous system activity and micro-arousal during sleep.

103) Drug given for maturation of fetal lung
   a. Betamethasone
   b. Hydrocortisone
   c. Indomethacin
   d. Prednisolone

Ans: (a)

The pulmonary system is among the last of the fetal organ systems to mature, both functionally and structurally. Antenatal corticosteroid therapy leads to improvement in neonatal lung function by enhancing maturational changes in lung architecture and by inducing lung enzymes involved in respiratory function. Antenatal corticosteroid therapy reduces the incidence of respiratory distress syndrome, intraventricular hemorrhage, necrotizing enterocolitis, sepsis, and neonatal mortality by approximately 50 percent.

Antenatal corticosteroids are recommended for pregnant woman who are at 23+0 to 33+6 weeks of gestation and at increased risk of preterm delivery within the next one to seven days. A course of antenatal corticosteroids consists of betamethasone suspension 12 mg intramuscularly every 24 hours for two doses or four doses of 6 mg dexamethasone intramuscularly 12 hours apart.

Neonatal benefits begin to accrue within a few hours of corticosteroid administration. Maximum efficacy occurs when delivery occurs two to seven days after administration of the first dose of antenatal corticosteroids. Efficacy is incomplete <24 hours from administration and appears to decline after 7 days.

104) False about respiratory distress syndrome in new-born
   a. Severe hypoxemia
   b. Presents within 2 to 7 days of birth
   c. Reticulonodular shadow on chest X-ray
   d. Use nasal continuous positive airway pressure in spontaneously breathing premature infants

   Ans: (b)

Respiratory distress syndrome (RDS) is a common problem in preterm infants. RDS is caused primarily by deficiency of pulmonary surfactant in an immature lung. Surfactant deficiency causes alveolar collapse leading to low lung compliance and volume and ventilation and perfusion mismatch resulting in hypoxemia. Other contributing factors to lung injury include inflammation and pulmonary edema.

RDS presents within the first minutes or hours of birth with signs of respiratory distress, such as tachypnea, nasal flaring, expiratory grunting, chest retractions, and cyanosis. Typically, RDS progresses over the first 48 to 72 hours of life with increased respiratory distress and begins to resolve after 72 hours. The use of antenatal steroids, exogenous surfactant, and/or continuous positive airway pressure dramatically improves pulmonary function and shortens the clinical course.

Chest radiographs of a new-born infant with respiratory distress syndrome reveal bilateral, diffuse, reticular granular or ground-glass appearances; air bronchograms; and poor lung expansion. See the x-ray below. The prominent air bronchograms represent aerated bronchioles superimposed on a background of collapsed alveoli.

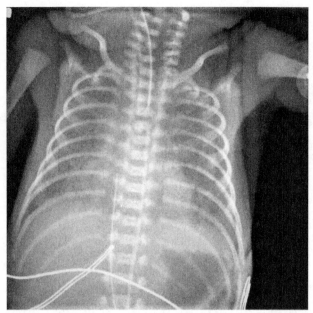

Bell-shaped thorax is due to generalized under-aeration. Lung volume is reduced, the lung parenchyma has a fine granular pattern, and peripherally extending air bronchograms are present.

In the delivery room, nasal continuous positive airway pressure (CPAP) is often used in spontaneously breathing premature infants immediately after birth as a potential alternative to immediate intubation and surfactant replacement.

Neonates with respiratory distress syndrome who require assisted ventilation with a fraction of inspiratory oxygen (FIO2) of more than 0.40 should receive intratracheal surfactant as soon as possible, preferably within 2 hours after birth.

105) Indication for lung transplantation
   a. Emphysema
   b. Primary pulmonary hypertension
   c. Cystic fibrosis
   d. All

Ans: (d)

Lung transplantation is a therapeutic consideration for many patients with nonmalignant end-stage lung disease. The most common diseases that lead to lung transplant are chronic obstructive pulmonary disease, interstitial lung disease, cystic fibrosis, alpha-1 antitrypsin deficiency, and idiopathic pulmonary arterial hypertension.

106) Silicosis is due to exposure in ------------ industry
   a. Granite quarrying
   b. Coal
   c. Paint
   d. Refinery

   Ans: (a)

Silicosis refers to a spectrum of pulmonary diseases caused by inhalation of free crystalline silica (silicon dioxide). Silicon dioxide is the predominant component of the Earth's crust. Silica sand is inexpensive, accessible, and versatile. Therefore, millions of workers throughout the world are at risk of disease. Workers in a broad range of industries (eg, sandblasting; granite quarrying; mining; masonry, foundry work, cement manufacturing, glass and ceramic manufacturing) are exposed to silicon dioxide.

107) Cystic fibrosis is associated with all except -
   a. Meconium ileus
   b. Metabolic acidosis
   c. Pneumonia
   d. Infertility

   Ans: (b)

Cystic fibrosis is caused by defects in the cystic fibrosis gene. This gene codes for a protein transmembrane conductance regulator (CFTR). CFTR protein functions as a chloride channel that is regulated by cAMP. Mutations in the CFTR gene result in abnormalities of cAMP-regulated chloride transport across epithelial cells on mucosal surfaces. Relative impermeability of epithelial cells to chloride ion is the primary defect.

137

Meconium ileus is the presenting problem in 10 to 20 percent of newborns with CF. 80 to 90 percent of infants with meconium ileus have CF.

Pulmonary involvement occurs in 90% of patients surviving the neonatal period. End-stage lung disease is the principal cause of death. Clinical manifestations include productive cough, wheezing, chronic bronchitis and recurrent pneumonias, progressive obstructive airways disease, exercise intolerance, dyspnea, and hemoptysis.

More than 95 percent of men with CF are infertile because of defects in sperm transport, although spermatogenesis is not affected.

108) Inspiratory stridor is seen in carcinoma of-
   a. Supraglottis
   b. Subglottis
   c. Glottis
   d. Trachea

Ans: (b)

Stridor is an abnormal, high-pitched sound produced by turbulent airflow through a partially obstructed upper airway (at the level of the supraglottis, glottis, subglottis, or trachea). Stridor may be inspiratory (most common), expiratory, or biphasic.
- Inspiratory stridor suggests a laryngeal obstruction
- Expiratory stridor implies tracheobronchial obstruction
- Biphasic stridor suggests a subglottic or glottic anomaly

Malignant Tumors of the Larynx
The larynx is divided into the supraglottic larynx, the glottic larynx, and the subglottic larynx. See the figure below.

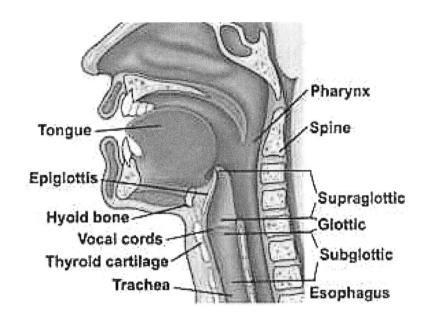

Common sites of origin are the true vocal cords (glottis) and the supraglottic larynx. Supraglottic tumors may not alter laryngeal function until they reach a relatively large size, at which time airway obstruction may be the first symptom. Conversely, glottic tumors alter voice quality early in their development and are thus often discovered at an early stage. The least common site is the subglottic larynx, where only 1% of primary laryngeal cancers originate. The origin of most cancers in this area is the glottic cancer that extends into the subglottic region. The delayed diagnosis is due to the lack of symptoms in the early stage of the disease and the hidden location of the tumor. The presenting symptoms are usually dyspnea and stridor. Direct laryngoscopy is essential for early detection of the tumor and the use of CT and MRI is advocated.

109) Pulmonary hypertension with prominent plexiform lesion:
(Multiple correct answers)
   a. Recurrent thromboemboli
   b. Interstitial lung disease
   c. Idiopathic pulmonary arterial hypertension
   d. Congenital heart disease with left-to-right shunts
   e. Pulmonary hypertension associated with HIV infection

Ans: (c, d, e)

Pulmonary hypertension (PH) is defined as a mean pulmonary arterial pressure more than 25 mm Hg at rest measured by invasive monitoring. The WHO classifies patients with PH into five groups based upon etiology:

1. Group 1 – Pulmonary arterial hypertension (PAH)
2. Group 2 – PH due to left heart disease
3. Group 3 – PH due to chronic lung disease and/or hypoxemia
4. Group 4 – Chronic thromboembolic pulmonary hypertension (CTEPH)
5. Group 5 – PH due to unclear multifactorial mechanisms

The term PAH is used to describe those included in group 1, while the term PH is used when describing all five groups.

Pulmonary arterial hypertension (PAH) is defined as PH with normal left-sided filling pressure (ie, pulmonary capillary wedge pressure < 15 mm Hg) and an increased PVR (> 3 units). Schistosomiasis is the most common cause of PAH worldwide; in regions of the world without endemic schistosomiasis, over half of cases of PAH are idiopathic (IPAH) and up to 10 percent are heritable (HPAH).

Idiopathic pulmonary arterial hypertension (IPAH) and heritable pulmonary arterial hypertension (HPAH) are disorders intrinsic to the pulmonary vascular bed that is characterized by sustained elevations in pulmonary arterial pressure and vascular resistance that generally lead to RV failure and death.

Pathological changes

PAH is a vasculopathy, characterized by vasoconstriction, cell proliferation, fibrosis, and microthrombosis. The seat of the disease in IPAH is in the small pulmonary arteries (between 40 and 100 μm in diameter) and arterioles.

- Grade I and II changes are characterized by muscularization of the small pulmonary arterioles, followed by medial hypertrophy and intimal hyperplasia.

- Grade III abnormalities are characterized by collagenous replacement of intimal cells, leading to an "onion-skin" appearance.
- Grade IV through VI abnormalities overlap and include plexiform lesions.

Grade IV through VI lesions are associated with a poor outcome in patients that undergo surgery for congenital shunts. See figure below.

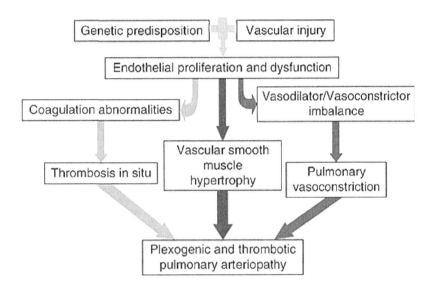

Plexogenic pulmonary arteriopathy is an arterial disease that develops in individuals with long standing pulmonary hypertension. Plexiform lesions are aneurysmatic dilations of a muscular artery that can occur in very small arteries and arterioles. The plexiform lesions contain collections of proliferating endothelial and smooth muscle cells, together with myofibroblasts and matrix proteins that can partially or completely occlude the vessel lumen. Narrowing or complete obliteration of the parent vessel by intimal thickening is a frequent associated finding, as is destruction of its media. Plexiform lesions often coexist with other obliterative vascular changes such as concentric laminar intimal thickening. These lesions are often found in patients with IPAH, but they also occur in the lungs of patients with severe PAH associated with left-to-right cardiac shunts, HIV infection, liver cirrhosis, and scleroderma. See figure below.

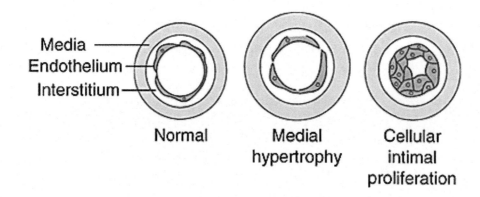

Media —
Endothelium —
Interstitium —

Normal　　　Medial　　　Cellular
　　　　　hypertrophy　　intimal
　　　　　　　　　　　proliferation

Adjacent　　Arteritis　　Plexiform　　Organized
normal and　　　　　　　lesion　　　thrombus
abnormal

Vascular lesions in idiopathic pulmonary arterial hypertension.
Plexogenic arteriopathy is the histologic hallmark of idiopathic
pulmonary arterial hypertension; it is seen in approximately 75% of
cases.

110)　True about granulomatosis with polyangiitis: Multiple Correct
　　　Answers
　　　　a.　Far more common among white individuals
　　　　b.　Oral ulcers
　　　　c.　Mainly involves small & medium sized vessels
　　　　d.　Lung involvement
　　　　e.　Kidney involvement

Ans:　(a, b, c, d, e)

Granulomatosis with polyangiitis (GPA), formerly known as Wegener granulomatosis, is a rare multisystem autoimmune disease of unknown etiology. Its hallmark features include necrotizing granulomatous inflammation and pauci-immune vasculitis in small- and medium-sized blood vessels.

Classic GPA involves the upper respiratory tract, lungs, and kidneys. Distinctive features may also occur in the eyes, ears, and other organs. 90% of patients with GPA have nasal involvement, including crusting, bleeding, and obstruction.

The three pathology hallmarks of GPA

1. Granulomatous inflammation in the upper or lower respiratory tract,
2. Necrotizing vasculitis affecting arteries or veins, and
3. Segmental glomerulonephritis.

Diagnostic criteria for GPA

1. Nasal or oral inflammation (painful or painless oral ulcers, or purulent or bloody nasal discharge)
2. Abnormal chest radiograph showing nodules, fixed infiltrates, or cavities
3. Abnormal urinary sediment (microscopic hematuria with or without red cell casts)
4. Granulomatous inflammation on biopsy of an artery or perivascular area

The presence of two or more of these four criteria yield a sensitivity and a specificity of 90 percent.

Cytoplasmic antineutrophil cytoplasmic antibody (c-ANCA) directed against PR3 is most specific for GPA

REFERENCES

1. www.uptodate.com
2. Ganong's Review of Medical Physiology, 26e
3. Pulmonary Physiology, 9e
4. Fishman's Pulmonary Diseases and Disorders, 5e
5. Murray and Nadel's Textbook of Respiratory Medicine, 6e
6. Harrison's Principles of Internal Medicine, 20e
7. Goldman-Cecil Medicine, 26e
8. Felson's Principles of Chest Roentgenology, 5e
9. Muller's Imaging of the Chest, 2e
10. Principles and Practice of Mechanical Ventilation, 3e
11. Tintinalli's Emergency Medicine: A Comprehensive Study Guide, 9e
12. Principles of Critical Care, 4e

Printed in Great Britain
by Amazon

21797172R00084